*Jesus, The Servant-Messiah*

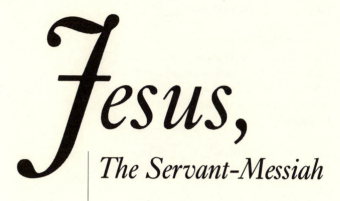

# Jesus,
## The Servant-Messiah

### MARINUS DE JONGE

Yale University Press
New Haven & London

Designed by Jill Breitbarth.
Set in Ehrhardt type by Keystone Typesetting, Inc.,
Orwigsburg, PA.
Printed in the United States of America by
BookCrafters, Chelsea, Michigan.

*Library of Congress Cataloging-in-Publication Data*
Jonge, Marinus de, 1925–
    Jesus, the Servant-Messiah / Marinus de Jonge.
        p.    cm.
    "Grew out of the Shaffer lectures delivered at
the Yale Divinity School in February 1989"—Pref.
    Includes bibliographical references and index.
    ISBN 0-300-04849-1
    1. Jesus Christ—Messiahship.  2. Jesus
Christ—Servanthood.  3. Jesus Christ—History
of doctrines—Early church, ca. 30–600.  4. Jesus
Christ—Historicity.  5. Jesus Christ—Knowledge
of his own divinity.  6. Bible. N.T. Gospels—
Criticism, interpretation, etc.  I. Title.  II. Title:
Shaffer lectures.
BT230.J7813  1991
232′.1—dc20                  90-47548
                                  CIP

10  9  8  7  6  5  4  3  2  1

# Contents

# *Preface*

This book picks up where my *Christology in Context: The Earliest Christian Response to Jesus* (1988) left off. In that book I concentrated on the various forms of early Christian response to Jesus; here I focus on Jesus himself, on the way he viewed his relationship to God and his mission. I have looked consistently for elements of continuity between the early Christian interpretations of Jesus' death and resurrection and his disciples' response to him before those crucial events.

The problem of "the historical Jesus," including that of reconstructing his own "Christology," is highly complicated because the nature of the sources at our disposal precludes definitive solutions. Yet we cannot let the matter rest; we must review earlier approaches and seek new openings. This book is a contribution to an ongoing discussion—as was my earlier collection of essays *Jesus: Inspiring and Disturbing Presence* (1974). It deals with a number of central historical and theological issues that will, I trust, be of interest to people beyond the circle of professional exegetes of the New Testament and historians of early Christianity.

This volume grew out of the Shaffer Lectures I delivered at the Yale Divinity School in February 1989. Its title reflects that of the Shaffer Lectures for 1939 given by T. W. Manson, later published as *The Servant-Messiah: A Study of the Public Ministry of Jesus* (1953). Because Manson's book has exercised considerable influence, especially in the English-speaking world, this study enters into discussion specifically

vii

with it. Comparison of the two books will show how much has changed in New Testament scholarship over the past fifty years.

I wish to thank Leander E. Keck and his colleagues at the Yale Divinity School for inviting me to present the Shaffer Lectures and all my friends in New Haven for the hospitality extended to my wife and me. I am also grateful for the encouraging and critical remarks received from many colleagues with whom I discussed the content of this book (or essential parts of it) in my own university in Leiden, at Yale, Princeton Theological Seminary, the University of Notre Dame, and the University of Iowa. A special word of thanks is due to Wayne A. Meeks, who read an expanded draft of the original lectures before they were delivered, to Charles Grench, executive editor at Yale University Press, who made very helpful comments on that version, and to Theresia Heesterman-Visser. Caroline Murphy, manuscript editor, gave valuable assistance in shaping the final text.

# I

## *The Earliest Christian Response to Jesus*

My book on early Christology, published in 1988 with the programmatic title *Christology in Context: The Earliest Christian Response to Jesus,*[1] contains a chapter entitled "The One with Whom It All Began." It is the last chapter, not the first, and it is relatively short (nine pages). I did not place this chapter on Jesus at the beginning because the sources from which we try to determine Jesus' views of his relationship with God and his mission to Israel and humanity are the very same as those from which we derive our knowledge of early Christology in its various forms and in the various stages of its development. These sources (and the earlier sources and traditions they incorporate) must be taken seriously as expressions of the faith of Jesus' followers. Hence twelve chapters on early Christology first, before turning to the one who sparked it all.

But do our sources permit us to trace certain lines backward in time, from the first stages in the richly variegated Christology of early Christian writings to the time before Jesus' death and, indeed, to Jesus' own views on his mission? In this book I will argue that, as complex and difficult as this undertaking is, we must make the attempt. However much early Christians were influenced and conditioned by the ideas of their environment and by the situation in which they found themselves many years after Jesus' mission, it was Jesus they spoke about and to him they assigned a pivotal role in God's dealings with humanity. All early Christology is in one way or another a response to Jesus. If we want to do justice to the early Christian message about Jesus, we must speak about Jesus' own teaching, including his teaching about himself, and about the response it evoked among his followers in Galilee and Jerusalem during his public appearances.[2]

The early Christians perceived a continuity between their belief in Jesus as the Christ, the Son of God and the Savior of the world, and Jesus' own ideas and intentions. Had this not been so, they would not have accorded him a central place in their conceptions of God's activity in human history and in their own lives. But critical historical research shows not only continuity but also development, even divergence, in early Christology. A similar dual strand is evident between the periods before and after Jesus' death. To what degree did the belief of early Christians in the resurrection of the master, who had been crucified but vindicated by God, intensify and modify their views of Jesus and the salvation he brought? Are we able to distinguish between early Christian Christology and Jesus' own?

## THE NATURE OF OUR SOURCES

Our answers to these questions depend to a large extent on our assessment of the results of the literary criticism and form criticism pursued by earlier generations of New Testament scholars.[3]

A few words on literary criticism of the synoptic gospels may suffice. As in my earlier book, I assume here that Mark is our oldest gospel and that the material common to Matthew and Luke goes back to a shared source known as Q. In addition, Mark very likely had access to an existing passion narrative, but such a narrative is extremely difficult to reconstruct. It is also far from easy to determine the exact wording, content, and arrangement of Q, although it can be demonstrated that this document consisted of a collection of sayings of Jesus and relevant material connected with them. Of course, some material found only in Matthew and Luke, and even individual pieces of tradition recorded only in the Fourth Gospel, may also go back to an earlier date. Yet in practice we shall do well to start with what is preserved in Mark and Q, paying special attention to the instances in which these two sources agree; the other material can be treated as corroborative evidence.

Form criticism traditionally concentrated on the period of oral transmission of the text units incorporated in the synoptic gospels. It tried to define and classify typical standard "forms" (such as several types of anecdotes and other short stories, as well as sayings of Jesus, clearly intended to convince people of the truth of the Christian message or to teach them to live as Christians in a hostile world). These forms were connected with specific situations, called *Sitze im Leben*, in the life of the early communities—for example, missionary activity, polemics, instruction of new members, other forms of teaching and preaching, baptism, and celebration of the "table of the Lord."

At a later stage, form criticism was also applied to the other writings of the New Testament. In particular, it has helped us discover liturgical material, hymns, prayers, doxologies (liturgical formulas of praise), and acclamations, as well as short formulations of faith, in the letters of Paul, the earliest written documents of Christianity. This has enabled us to distinguish a great number of traditional formulas and patterns of thought expressing the meaning of Jesus' death and resurrection and of his mission in God's dealings with Israel and the world. There is clearly a great variety even at the beginning. Some of the statements Paul incorporates are clearly pre-Pauline; others are not typically Pauline but represent the common faith of Paul and the people he addressed. It is interesting to compare what is found in this layer of tradition—the oldest to have been reconstructed with any certainty—with the traditions about Jesus' teaching and actions that are common to Mark and Q.[4]

It is very problematic, however, to apply the results of form-critical analysis to questions of historicity: material was transmitted not so much because the need was felt to record historical fact but because this material spoke to the questions and needs of the early followers of Jesus after his resurrection. There is no doubt that oral transmission shapes and transforms. Inferring from what Matthew and Luke did with material taken over from Mark and Q, we can safely assume that changes and adaptations were also made freely in the period before things were written down. If the original tradition consisted of stories about Jesus and individual sayings, and if the only coherent narrative of early origin was that of the passion and crucifixion, what reason is there to suppose that the sketchy outline of Jesus' public activities found in Mark was known before him?

Form criticism has so complicated the search for the historical Jesus

that many scholars are understandably reluctant to reach back beyond
the meaning and function of traditions preserved in the early communities. We know nothing about Jesus that has not been handed down to
us by his followers after Easter. All we have bears the stamp of the life,
teaching, and preaching of the earliest Christian communities; references to him by non-Christian authors are all later and not very specific.[5] It behooves us then, to proceed with extreme caution—but also
to consider how a number of well-known scholars have approached the
search.

## THE QUEST OF THE HISTORICAL JESUS

### T. W. Manson, *The Servant-Messiah*

Representative of much sober and solid British scholarship
immediately before and after World War II is T. W. Manson's book *The
Servant-Messiah*, mentioned in the preface.

Manson expresses considerable skepticism about form criticism.[6]
He does not deny that it may be useful for describing literary forms, but
he has doubts about the form critics' attempts to relate these forms to
specific socio-historical contexts. However much the tradition of stories
and sayings may have been influenced by the circumstances and needs
of the Christian communities of the first century of the Common Era,
we should be prepared to look for the *Sitz im Leben* first in the Jewish
culture or in the life of Jesus, he argues, and not resort automatically to a
*Sitz im Leben* in the early church. Moreover, what we do know about the
tradition process in the early church does not confirm the opinion of the
form critics that many sayings of Jesus or stories about him were altered
or constructed in view of the needs of the various early Christian
groups. "The Pauline letters abound in utterances which could readily
be transferred to the faithful as oracles of the Lord. But how many are?"
(p. 214).

Another of Manson's objections to form criticism is its full-scale
attack on the Markan framework. Why, Manson asks, should the need
for a connected story of Jesus' ministry have arisen in the sixties, when
the Gospel of Mark was composed, but not during the thirty-odd years
before, apart from a passion narrative? And is it really plausible that
during that interval the details of the story were remembered but the

general outline forgotten? "I am increasingly convinced," he writes in 1954, "that the Marcan story presents in the main an orderly and logical development; and that this development or framework has as good a title to be considered reliable historical material as any particular anecdote incorporated in it" (p. 213).

In chapters 3 and 4 of *The Servant-Messiah*, Manson poses two simple questions: What did Jesus do? and Why did he do it? For the answer to the first question he relies mainly on Mark; for the second, on the sayings source Q—in his eyes "the earliest manual of instruction for the converted" (p. 52). The apostolic kerygma in Paul's letters and in the speeches in Acts does not merely hang in the air but is founded on reliable information about Jesus' convictions and corresponding actions.[7] Jesus' words and deeds cannot be separated but have to be studied together.

Much of Manson's criticism of the form critics is to the point. We know very little about the circumstances in which the various strands of early Christianity arose, and we should be cautious in reconstructing the *Sitz im Leben* of specific sayings and stories and in tracing their origin and development. A *Sitz im Leben* in the early church does not preclude an earlier one in the life of Jesus, and it is important to remember that Jesus and his first followers were Jews. Manson and many others have rightly criticized R. Bultmann for devoting some hundred-twenty pages of his *Theology of the New Testament*[8] to the Hellenistic Christian congregations but a mere thirty to Jesus and another thirty to the earliest Palestinian church.[9]

Yet it is also clear that Manson did not take seriously enough the fact that the only reliable information we have about Jesus was transmitted by his disciples after his death, believed to have been followed by his resurrection, and that it was transmitted for the benefit of the congregations of early Christians. Now we have "Jesus in the church's gospels" and we meet "Jesus of Nazareth in New Testament preaching," to mention the titles of two more recent studies.[10] And if Manson, relying on Mark, claims to have been able to reconstruct an intelligible, consistent, and credible story of Jesus' ministry, he has at the most reconstructed Mark's story, supplemented by a number of details taken from Q. It is not that we should disbelieve Mark or start from the supposition that he has given a wrong or extremely biased picture, distorting the evidence at his disposal. But we should realize that we can never separate with absolute certainty the genuine words of Jesus from the constructions of the evangelists after him or the tradition before them. We know Jesus only as the disciples remembered him.

Manson's main contribution to present-day research on the historical Jesus is his insistence that Jesus and the movement sparked by him should be studied in the context of the political, social, economic, and religious life of contemporary Judaism and within the framework of Hellenistic culture and of the Roman empire of his day. We can say nothing substantial about Jesus' teachings or the kerygma of the early church (or indeed about early Christology in general) without paying close attention to the expectations cherished by Jesus' Jewish contemporaries concerning God's decisive intervention in the history of Israel and of the entire world.

*The Servant-Messiah* begins with an eminently readable chapter on the situation in Palestine and the messianic hope of first-century Jews. Though it is somewhat dated now, the essential point is well made that Jewish messianic ideals are misunderstood when they are termed "materialistic" or "purely practical" or "this-worldly" (p. 9): "If Israel could be one hundred percent Israel, enjoying all the privileges and shouldering all the responsibilities of their position, the purpose of God would be realized: the Kingdom of God would be a reality" (pp. 9–10).

John the Baptist, whom Manson characterizes as "the messianic herald" in his second chapter, must be viewed in this context. John delivered the first hard blow to the comfortable belief that "the immediate beneficiaries of this God-given Messianic victory are the people of Israel: the children of Abraham" (p. 37). His message is a clear call to moral renewal in view of the imminent judgment on Israel and the inauguration of God's Kingdom. Yet John, in all his radicalism and severity, remained within the boundaries of Jewish beliefs and Jewish expectations. To Manson he is a tragic figure: "For his was the last supreme effort to make an unworkable system work" (p. 49).

Manson attempts to show that Jesus' challenge to current Jewish ideals and hopes was much more incisive and thoroughgoing than John's. His whole messianic ministry—his teaching, his acts, and finally his death on the cross—is a repudiation of those beliefs. Manson's reconstruction of Jesus' ministry, based on the sequence of events sketched in Mark and on the comments found in Jesus' sayings collected in Q, cannot be accepted without careful scrutiny. But he highlights a number of aspects of Jesus' teaching that have been taken up by other scholars and that will also receive due attention in the following chapters of this book.

Thus he stresses correctly that, by befriending "publicans and sinners" and by criticizing current religious practice, Jesus came into conflict with Jewish authorities. "So it came about that Jesus not only had to challenge the existing messianic dreams in the name of the Kingdom of God, he had also to question the validity of Torah and tradition as the final expression of the will of God, and that in the name of his own Ministry, which for him is the rule of God" (pp. 60–61). According to Manson, Jesus was faced not only with the opposition of Jewish leaders and the suspicion of the Galilean tetrarch Herod Antipas but also with the patriotic zeal of his followers. The dramatic episode at Caesarea Philippi, with Peter's confession of Jesus as the Messiah followed by Jesus' prediction of his own suffering and resurrection (Mark 8:27–9:1), marks a turning point both in the story as Mark tells it and in the historical relationship between Jesus and his disciples. Combining the picture of the feeding of the five thousand in Mark 6:33–56 with the note in John 6:15 that the people were about to make Jesus king, Manson concludes that Jesus' subsequent journeys in Tyre and Sidon were "a flight from the dangerous enthusiasm of his friends" rather than "from the suspicions and fears of his enemies" (p. 71).

Manson brings out with admirable clarity what Mark wants to tell his readers. The question of Jesus' messiahship and its reinterpretation in light of his suffering and crucifixion was a hot issue in early Christianity, possibly even before Jesus' death. Yet we cannot take for granted that things happened more or less as Mark reports them.

Among the events in Jerusalem reported by Mark, Manson pays special attention to the cleansing of the Temple, an action that heightens the tension and provokes further opposition to Jesus. Mark's account (11:15–19) stresses that "the Messiah, instead of clearing the Gentiles out of the Holy City, bag and baggage, makes his first public act the vindication of Gentile rights in the Temple itself" (p. 83).[11] Manson gives short shrift to the proceedings before the Sanhedrin, in his eyes to be regarded not as a formal trial but as an informal inquiry.

He thinks that Jesus did admit openly before the Sanhedrin that he regarded himself as the Messiah. He stood for the Kingdom of God, he *was* the Kingdom of God, he was the Messiah. "So Jesus went to the Cross—and made it his everlasting throne" (p. 88).

The synoptic gospels placed the announcement of "the Kingdom of God" at the center of Jesus' message; hence, what Jesus meant by this expression occupies a central place in reconstructions of his life and teaching. Albert Schweitzer[12] had emphasized that Jesus announced the coming of God's Kingdom in the very near future, after a short period of distress; his disciples would not even have time to reach all the cities in Israel with this message (Matt. 10:23). When this apocalyptic prediction did not come true, Jesus recognized that it was his duty to suffer and die for others so as to make it possible for the Kingdom to come.

This picture was not acceptable to Manson, or to most other British scholars of his day. "The ministry of Jesus is not a prelude to the Kingdom of God," he maintains: "it *is* the Kingdom of God." Drawing on C. H. Dodd's concept of "realized eschatology,"[13] Manson takes issue with Schweitzer and with F. C. Burkitt's remark that Jesus saw his own career as a prologue to the King Messiah, who would come in glory on the clouds of heaven to judge the world and to vindicate the elect of God. In "The Life of Jesus" he comments:

> "The Prologue of which Burkitt speaks in fact makes nonsense of the expected sequel; so much so that it is no calamity but a positive relief that there is no Parousia of the conventional Jewish pattern. . . . The most significant thing about the Jesus of the eschatological theory, the permanent effective thing right down to the life of Schweitzer himself, is the non-eschatological, even the anti-eschatological element. The interior ethic is the abiding moral force: the Prologue has become the whole drama." (p. 217)

Jesus' mission can be properly understood only in the context of Jewish eschatological expectations. On this Schweitzer and the great majority of modern scholars, including Manson, agree. But Manson's view of the nature of the Kingdom in Jesus' teaching is at least as one-sided as Schweitzer's. He is wrong in saying that "the Kingdom is not something to be added to the Ministry, it is already present in the

Ministry. The sacrifice and suffering of the Son of man are not the prelude to triumph; properly understood they are the supreme triumph" (p. 77).

I shall return to this central issue later, but it is appropriate to stress even here that any interpretation of the death of Jesus, preacher *and* inaugurator of the Kingdom, requires reflection on God's vindication of this supreme servant. Also that Jesus, in speaking about the Kingdom, must have shared the Jewish view that God's sovereign rule will some day encompass all creation and require the obedience of all human beings. If God is truly God, there must be a final judgment and a final triumph affecting the entire creation.

Characteristic of Manson's approach is his view of Jesus as Servant. Commenting on the temptation narrative in Q (Matt. 4:1–11, par. Luke 4:1–13), which he regards as a "spiritual experience of Jesus thrown into parabolic narrative form for the instruction of his disciples" (p. 55), he remarks that in all Jesus' responses to the devil in this story, God is put in the center of the stage. Everything revolves around God's Kingdom. He adds: "The Messiah is only God's servant—indeed just because he is Messiah he must be preeminently God's servant!" (p. 57). Later, when dealing with Jesus as the Son of man predicted in Daniel, Manson stresses that "Jesus defines the Son of man in terms of the Servant of the Lord portrayed in Isaiah 40–55" (p. 73). Typical of Manson is his emphasis on "Son of man" as a "corporate personality," a group of people represented by an individual figure. Jesus is the Son of man par excellence; he finally stands alone, "embodying in his own person the perfect human response to the regal claims of God."[14] Jesus recognized that his suffering and sacrifice were the inevitable outcome of his supreme obedience to God.

Here, again, Manson has pointed to a very important issue. Jesus' enigmatic designation of himself as "Son of man" has led to much discussion, and there is no consensus in the matter. Manson's emphasis on the influence of Daniel 7 is shared by many; his contention that not only here but also in the gospels "Son of man" may have a collective meaning is not. There has also been much debate on the influence of the Deutero-Isaianic Servant Songs on the thinking of Jesus and the early Church. Many doubt whether it has been so extensive as Manson thinks. I shall return to this below.

### N. A. Dahl, "The Problem of the Historical Jesus"

In retrospect, *The Servant-Messiah* may be said to mark the end of an era. After R. Bultmann, a central figure among the form critics of the gospels, had declared categorically, "I do indeed think that we can know almost nothing concerning the life and personality of Jesus, since the early Christian sources show no interest in either, are moreover fragmentary and often legendary; and other sources about Jesus do not exist,"[15] the quest of the historical Jesus received little attention. A number of scholars in Great Britain, Manson among them, formed an exception to the rule.[16]

Around the time Manson's book was published, leading scholars in the school of Bultmann started what has since been termed the "new quest of the historical Jesus." It is usually considered to have begun with E. Käsemann's article "The Problem of the Historical Jesus" in 1954.[17] This new quest was motivated not so much by renewed historical curiosity as by theological interest; I shall come back to it in the next chapter.

Also at the same time (1952), N. A. Dahl gave a lecture at Uppsala on "The Problem of the Historical Jesus" in which he went his own way, independent of British scholarship and of developments in the school of Bultmann.[18] Some elements in his approach deserve our attention here.

Dahl reminds us that all our evidence has come down to us as recollections about Jesus[19] retained in the tradition of the Christian communities for which the proclamation of the risen Lord was the central element of faith. We should note the word "recollections" here; people wanted to be guided by what Jesus had said and done. Along with many others, Dahl is of the opinion that form criticism "has not yielded objective criteria for separating older from later traditions to the degree expected" (p. 65). Sayings varied in the tradition, and kept varying, because they were handed down as words of the living Lord to his communities in their current circumstances. They were transmitted because they remained relevant.

A clear differentiation between pure history and later theology is impossible. Yet, in Dahl's opinion, "the gospel tradition permits us to draw a very clear picture of what was typical and characteristic of Jesus" (p. 67). He suggests that we make cross sections of the tradition and analyze sayings and reports of differing form and genre, transmitted in various layers of the tradition. In so doing we will find a number of linking characteristics, such as Jesus' proclamation of the Kingdom of God, his position with respect to the Law, and his attitude toward various groups in society.

The cross-section method should be supplemented, Dahl suggests, by drawing longitudinal lines leading from Judaism through the figure of Jesus to primitive Christianity. "The historical Jesus is to be found at the crossroads where Christianity and Judaism begin separating from each other although it only became gradually clear that the paths parted in such a way that Christianity appeared as a new religion alongside Judaism" (p. 68). In other words, we must view Jesus in the context of the Palestinian Judaism of his day and at the same time work backward from the various formulations of primitive Christianity toward the man who is at their center.

Dahl's way out of the impasse created by the nature of our sources is valuable. He does not need to rely on Mark in order to have a framework for arranging individual traditions, nor does he need to assume or to prove the historicity of individual sayings or anecdotes. His cross-section method, called by others the "criterion of multiple attestation,"[20] guarantees at least a reasonable degree of certainty about a number of common characteristics. His complementary longitudinal approach gives us the possibility to broaden our scope. It allows us both to compare developments in contemporary Judaism and relate them to opinions and attitudes attributed to Jesus and to examine the notions current in early Christianity and surmise to what extent they originated in what Jesus said and did during his public ministry.

Dahl calls for radical criticism. The genuineness of each individual piece of tradition is to be demonstrated, not the non-genuineness (as some more conservative critics have argued). On the one hand, there is the minimum requirement, which is now often called "the criterion of dissimilarity":[21] what can be neither derived from Judaism nor attributed to primitive Christianity can be considered to go back to Jesus. Dahl (and many others) is right in warning us that this is only one heuristic principle among others, though, and yields only the barest minimum. It excludes all that Jesus shared with his fellow Jews and all that primitive Christianity took over from its master. Dahl, therefore, adds a maximum requirement: "On the other hand, the total tradition concerning Jesus must be taken into consideration. In its totality it is theology of the Church, and at the same time it is also in its totality a reflex of Jesus' activity—a *maximum* which contains everything of importance for our historical knowledge about Jesus" (p. 71). Our task is to narrow as much as possible the gap between the maximum of the tradition and the critically ensured minimum. It will not be possible to reconstruct a biography of Jesus, and, because our sources are not interested in it, we know nothing of Jesus' inner life. But we can reconstruct a reasonably clear picture of the main lines of Jesus' mission and the essence of his teaching.

One final important point in Dahl's seminal article requires attention. All along he stresses the continuity between Jesus' message and that of the early church. Like Manson, Dahl takes up Albert Schweitzer's views on the eschatological message of Jesus. Correcting rather than criticizing this great scholar, he asserts that Jesus "preached that in and with his own mission, his word and his work, God's Kingdom was already breaking in. The primitive community and Paul share the same expectation, but their place in the eschatological history of salvation is different. . . . Between Jesus and the primitive community there lie his death and resurrection as decisive events: Jesus is appointed to the position of messianic ruler in which he shall some day be revealed" (p. 82). This continuity in expectation is essential for the relationship between the primitive church and Jesus. "Either the events of Easter and Pentecost are the preliminary fulfillment of Jesus' eschatological promise, or this promise, at the heart of his message, remained unfulfilled" (p. 83).

## G. N. Stanton and F. Hahn

Passing over the results of the new quest, to be discussed briefly in the next chapter, I now turn to two studies which appeared in the seventies. The first is a book by G. N. Stanton, *Jesus of Nazareth in*

*New Testament Preaching* (1974),[22] the second an article by F. Hahn entitled "Methodische Überlegungen zur Rückfrage nach Jesus," which appeared in the same year.[23] From both studies I shall take a few points that are of importance for the present inquiry.

Stanton gives an independent assessment of the evidence on the basis of a critical review of previous scholarship, including both the British tradition and the school of Bultmann. In his view, "the dual perspective of the gospel traditions is unescapable, they are kerygmatic and they intend to sketch out the life and character of Jesus. To by-pass or to minimise either aspect is to miss the finely-held balance of the traditions themselves" (p. 172). This double aspect allows us to draw upon the gospels in our search for the essential characteristics of Jesus' ministry.

Stanton emphasizes that Jesus proclaimed the Kingdom of God: God's eschatological rule was in some sense present in his ministry, for God was acting through Jesus in an entirely new way. This implied, for Jesus, associating with tax collectors and sinners, a conduct that brought him severe questioning by scribes and Pharisees. Jesus' interest in those who were shunned by society on account of their bodily ills and in women and children is likewise inseparable from his eschatological message. Many people objected to Jesus' message because his claims and promises were not accompanied by any outward signs of the realization of God's kingly rule. Hence Jesus' telling of the parables of growth, which in Stanton's view should be called parables of contrast. "Blessed is he who takes no offense at me," we read in Matt. 11:6 (par. Luke 7:23—a Q-saying). The scandal surrounding Jesus was part of the message of the early church, but it was already there during Jesus' preaching on earth.

The words, actions, and person of Jesus are closely interrelated. Stanton brings this out in an interesting analysis of the use of the term *Son of man* by Jesus in the gospels. One of his conclusions is that "the 'present' Son of man sayings, like Jesus' proclamation of the Kingdom, point to the scandal, the 'unexpectedness' of Jesus' character, but they also reflect his authority and his concern for those on the fringe of society" (p. 162). Thus, if Jesus saw himself as the obedient, faithful, yet rejected and suffering Son of man, he must have expected to be vindicated by God, just as the Kingdom of God now manifesting itself in Jesus' words and actions would soon be revealed in full strength and glory. Both concepts—the Kingdom of God and the Son of man—are directly related to Jesus' person.

Stanton's argument implies that, despite the clear differences between the situation of Jesus and his disciples before Good Friday and Easter and that of the community of believers afterward, there must have been more continuity than has often been thought. Stanton underscores this by referring to an article by H. Schürmann on the origins of the sayings tradition.[24] This scholar had pointed to a definite *Sitz im Leben* for the sayings of Jesus before Easter: the missionary preaching of his disciples, who announced the coming of the Kingdom and called for repentance. Sent out by Jesus, they could expect to be asked for their credentials; in presenting them, they must have referred to their master's words, and also to his actions. They must have reported significant deeds of Jesus, telling stories about him, and they must have continued to do so after Easter—until, much later, a selection of stories and sayings was finally included in the written sources now at our disposal.

F. Hahn's article brings together in an admirable fashion the principles of Jesus research in the post-Bultmannian era.[25] The key word is *Rückfrage* (asking backward). One cannot fully understand the teaching and preaching of the early church if one does not take seriously that it constantly refers back to Jesus, "asks back" to the time of his activity on earth. Jesus in his person not only provided the starting point of the Jesus tradition; he remained the center of it.

Hahn fully acknowledges and spells out how the tradition concerning Jesus was selected, molded, and interpreted anew by early Christians in view of its function in the preaching and teaching of the community. Nevertheless, the entire tradition known to us intends to hand down Jesus' words in the context of his actions and claims to present them in the right perspective. Hahn refers to a process of crystallization around a kernel of *ipsissima verba* and *ipsissima facta*. But it is impossible, he argues, and at the same time pointless to try to isolate this kernel by subtraction. In practice, neither the opposition "word of Jesus" versus "word formed by the community" nor the opposition "genuine" versus "non-genuine" is useful.

One cannot restrict oneself to the critically ensured minimum; there is also a maximum of potentially relevant material. Yet Hahn underlines the difficulty of applying criteria at all. Like the criterion of dissimilarity, the criterion of coherence (concentrating on what may be regarded as coherent with material that has been proved genuine) has deficiencies. And if we seek to supplement these two criteria with the criterion of multiple attestation, we should bear in mind that even sayings occurring in only one source may be genuine. Specific criteria like the use of Aramaic words or turns of speech frequently connected with Jesus are not completely reliable either.[26] Only by combining and subtly balancing various approaches can we hope to gain real insight.

As central elements in what he calls "the total picture of the pre-Easter history of Jesus" (pp. 40–51), Hahn mentions the following:

1) Jesus came into conflict with his fellow Jews because of his nonconformist views and conduct. He was not prepared to live in accordance with ideas and customs prevalent in contemporary Judaism but, rather, distinguished between human customs and God's will and was prepared even to question the regulations of the Torah in that light (Mark 10:2–12).

2) There was something radically new about Jesus, and those who followed him sensed this. It is expressed in his message of the coming of the kingdom of God, which is present in his words, his exorcisms and his healings, and his fellowship with socially undesirable elements. It is a dynamic reality aimed at encompassing the entire world in a not-too-distant future. People are confronted with final decisions traditionally associated with the final judgment. They are called upon to join Jesus and to become members of the eschatological community of his followers (not confined to the elect in Israel).

3) Jesus' authority and his claim on people are directly linked with his message about the new period visible, audible, and tangible in his words and actions—the Kingdom now dynamically present in this world. Asking people to make radical, definitive decisions, risking his life in a conflict with his adversaries, Jesus must have lived out of the certainty of a very special relationship to God, his Father. He must have regarded his life *and* his death in the light of the unique task commissioned to him by his Father.

## THE EARLIEST CHRISTOLOGY
## AS RESPONSE TO JESUS

This critical review of a number of important contributions to the quest of the historical Jesus[27] puts us in a position to assess various ways open to us in our search for Jesus' own views on his relationship to God and his role in God's dealings with the world.

To begin with, it has become very clear that the search for genuine sayings of Jesus and historical anecdotes about his public ministry is a very difficult one. Scholars have differed continually in their assessments of the gospel material and in their reconstructions of the sayings and stories of Jesus. We cannot dispense with this kind of investigation, but we should realize that it will never give us a satisfactory, let alone complete, picture of Jesus and of all he stood for.

We should view the early traditions about Jesus as recollections, as attempts to "ask back," as response. People looked for guidance from Jesus, whom they believed to be a living Lord; therefore, what he had said and done during his public ministry was of essential value to them. We shall have to study closely the ways in which sayings of Jesus, stories about Jesus, and other references to his work on earth were transmitted as relevant data in the various strands (and genres) of early Christian tradition.

It is appropriate to begin by comparing the oldest sources, Mark and Q, but also to take into account the potential value of material found only in Matthew, Luke, John, or Acts. The criterion of multiple attestation cannot be applied in an exclusive way. In my *Christology in Context* I emphasized that all living tradition presupposes constant change and adaptation, but also continuity—hence my use of the heading "Continuation and Development" to describe the later stages in the tradition.[28]

In particular, I would like to stress that in examining our oldest sources we should pay due attention to the early material in the letters of Paul. Admittedly, very few references to Jesus' earthly life and teaching have survived there—the entire emphasis is on his death and resurrection. In the cultic commemoration of the Last Supper there was a brief reference to the fact that the Lord was betrayed (1 Cor. 11:23–26); in 1 Thess. 2:14–16 the responsibility for the killing of Jesus (and of the prophets before him) is laid upon the Jews. Paul seldom refers to words of Jesus. The few references he does make to him (1 Cor. 7:10, 12, 25; 9:14), even when taken together with a number of allusions, do not give us much to go on. This has often been taken to mean that Paul was interested solely in the fact of Jesus' death and resurrection. But is it plausible that Paul, and the tradition before him, should really have spoken about Jesus' death "for us" and used this ancient formula in a hortatory context (Rom. 14:15; 1 Cor. 8:11; 2 Cor. 5:15) without having any further interest in or knowledge of the one who gave his life?[29]

Early Christianity could never have attached such a central value to what happened at the cross and have given voice to its certainty that Jesus had been raised from the dead in the ways it did without reliable knowledge about the Jesus who had died and the motives behind his words and actions. Without some continuity with the beliefs and expectations about Jesus before his death, and with his own convictions about himself, the early Christian kerygma about the meaning of his death and resurrection, and the preaching about salvation connected with it, remains inexplicable.

## "THE GOSPEL OF CHRIST"

The continuity in the understanding of Jesus before and after his crucifixion and resurrection can be illustrated by a brief review of the use of the term "the Gospel of Christ" (*to euaggelion tou Christou*) in the writings of the New Testament.[30] In the letters of Paul this term denotes the message concerning the Christ preached by him and by all other apostles. It is, most likely, a pre-Pauline expression in which "Christ" stands for the basic Christian belief about Jesus expressed in proclamations concerning his death and resurrection. In 1 Cor. 15:1–2 Paul introduces the ancient pre-Pauline formula about Jesus' death and resurrection, found in vv. 3–5, with the words: "I must remind you of the gospel that I preached to you; the gospel which you received. . . . Do you still hold fast the Gospel as I preached it to you?" (NEB).

Mark begins his book, which was later itself to receive the designation "gospel" (*euaggelion*), with the words, "The beginning of the gospel of Jesus Christ (the Son of God)."[31] For him the good news concerning Jesus Christ clearly includes the story of Jesus' activities in Galilee and

Jerusalem. He extends the term *euaggelion* to encompass the narrative of Jesus' ministry that begins with the appearance of John the Baptist and ends with Jesus' death and resurrection in Jerusalem. Mark, writing in the time just before and during the Jewish war against the Romans in 66–70 C.E., had to make clear in what sense Jesus could and should be called the Messiah; he could achieve his purpose only by relating the events that led up to Jesus' death on the cross and by showing what sort of person he was.

We may go back even farther. As mentioned earlier, it seems that Mark must have worked from an earlier passion narrative, though there is considerable disagreement about the scope and wording of this narrative. In any case a collection of stories about the events leading up to the crucifixion must have been in circulation. Such a collection could have been used to instruct new members of the Christian communities about what had happened and to make clear to outsiders that this crucified Jesus was not a criminal or a revolutionary but the Messiah expected by Israel. Celebrating communion in the inner circle in order to commemorate the Lord's death, one could simply refer to "the night he was betrayed" (1 Cor. 11:23–26). But more had to be said if one wanted to explain to the uninitiated why one believed in a Lord who had suffered such an ignominious death. It was not enough just to tell what happened at the end of Jesus' ministry; Mark and Q show that there was also a keen interest in the earlier stages of that ministry. Early Christians could not possibly limit themselves to the mere fact of Jesus' death followed, according to their conviction, by the resurrection. What mattered was that it was the death of Jesus, a man who had come with a new message, a decisive appeal on behalf of God, a call to repentance and discipleship—a man who had devoted himself completely to his mission and had been willing to give up his life for it. The kerygma in all its variation unfolds the message about (Jesus) Christ; this presupposes Jesus' own message in the context of his actions and integrated into his entire life.

Our oldest traditions also use the term *euaggelion* in connection with Jesus' own preaching of the Kingdom of God, commonly regarded as a core element in the ancient material about him.[32] In Mark 1:14–15 we read, "Now after John was arrested, Jesus came into Galilee, preaching the gospel of God, and saying: 'The time is fulfilled, and the Kingdom of God is at hand; repent, and believe in the gospel.'" These are the first words ascribed to Jesus in this gospel, formulated by Mark to summarize Jesus' message. As L. E. Keck points out, "this is almost universally acknowledged to be at the same time a formulation by the church and an accurate summary of what Jesus had to say."[33] We should note that also in Q Jesus is the one who preaches and inaugurates the Kingdom (see Luke 7:18–23, par. Matt. 11:2–6). At the climax of a series of allusions to prophecies from the Book of Isaiah in Luke 7:22 (par. Matt. 11:5) we encounter the verb *euaggelizesthai:* "the poor have good news preached to them." This is a clear reference to Isa. 61:1, which is quoted directly in Luke's description of Jesus' preaching in Nazareth (4:18). The first of the four beatitudes in Luke (6:20), which must have formed the beginning of Jesus' teaching in Q, is again addressed to the poor: "Blessed are you poor, for yours is the Kingdom of God." Jesus' proclamation in Mark 1:14 that "the kingdom of God is at hand" is reminiscent of Isa. 52:7, "How beautiful upon the mountains are the feet of him who brings good tidings, who publishes peace—who says to Zion, 'Your God reigns.'" We should add that Paul, too, knows the expression "the gospel of God" and uses it in prominent places, just as he uses an (adapted) quotation from Isa. 52:7 in Rom. 10:15, where he meditates on the essence of the Christian message (and uses traditional formulas in vv. 9 and 13).[34]

The agreement in terminology in the earliest tradition is remarkable. Jesus and those among his followers sent out as preachers bring the good news on behalf of God. For Mark and Q this good news is the announcement of God's reign. Mark sees Jesus' own message about the arrival of God's Kingdom as an integral part of "the gospel about Jesus Christ." The parables of the seed growing secretly (in Mark 4:26–29) and the mustard seed (in Mark 4:30–32) show the contrast between the modest beginning in the present and the glorious end in the future. In Q John the Baptist in his uncertainty is referred to what the disciples have seen and heard: Jesus' preaching, his healings, and his exorcisms mark the beginning of God's reign on earth (cf. Luke 11:20, par. Matt. 12:28). Therefore Jesus adds: "blessed is he who takes no offense at me" (Luke 7:18–23). At the same time Jesus promises that the poor will have a share in the Kingdom of God when it is fully realized on earth (Luke 6:20).

# II

*Theological*
*Considerations in*
*the Search for the*
*Historical Jesus*

One of the main contributions of Albert Schweitzer's *Quest of the Historical Jesus* was his demonstration of the close link between historical and theological motives behind the search for the real Jesus. Many scholars set out to find the original teacher of Nazareth, believing that he would be able to guide modern believers in a more inspiring and effective way than the Christ of the church. Others sought to defend traditional Christian tenets concerning Jesus Christ by proving the essential continuity between Jesus' own convictions and the beliefs of his followers or by disqualifying modern historical method as a means of describing those aspects of Jesus' ministry which, in their view, were intelligible only by assuming divine intervention.

Schweitzer also illustrated by many examples the perils of modernizing Jesus. Honest historical research will have to depict Jesus as a child of his own time. Schweitzer himself saw him as a prophet who expected the coming of the Kingdom in the very near future and who shared the apocalyptic ideas of his time, which are strange in the eyes of modern believers. Can one be a true follower of Jesus without sharing his concepts about the imminence and the nature of the Kingdom of God? For Schweitzer not these concepts but the will was important, and he drew his own consequences in becoming a doctor in Africa.[1]

The impasse in the quest of the historical Jesus in continental Europe during the period between the two world wars arose not only out of the complications encountered in form criticism but also out of theological uneasiness. Not only was the possibility of deriving reliable evidence from the sources at our disposal doubted, but also the advisability of collecting such evidence was seriously questioned. Karl Barth denied the possibility of connecting faith with any particular events in history, especially with events in the life of Jesus; such a connection, he argued, negated the very nature of faith. Faith is response, not to the results of historical investigation, but to the proclamation of a message. At least for the early Barth, the *Leben-Jesu-Forschung* was both in practice and in principle a fruitless and disastrous undertaking.[2]

We need to bear this in mind if we wish to understand why the analysis of the problem of the historical Jesus by Bultmann (whose theological views were originally akin to Barth's), first in his 1926 book on Jesus and later in the first section of his 1948 *Theology of the New Testament,* had such an enormous impact on New Testament scholarship—and on theology in general—until long after World War II. It combined a particular form of literary and historical criticism with an existentialist kerygmatic theology that clearly had a great appeal during a period of European history in which people experienced the shaking of all their foundations.

The kerygma challenges us, Bultmann contends; it reveals the possibility of a new existence to us and opens the door for us to enter into it. We are not allowed to rely on historical facts, nor are we made dependent on specific words and formulas. The latter would function merely as illicit objectifications of an existential truth that can be grasped by existential faith alone.

Describing Jesus' message in the very short section on Jesus in his *Theology of the New Testament,* Bultmann does not deny that Jesus' announcement of the Kingdom must be seen in the context of Jewish eschatological expectations. But in his proclamation of the Kingdom of God, Jesus emphasized the presence of the Kingdom in his own words and actions. Mark 1:15 is freely rendered as: "Now the time is come. God's reign is breaking in! The end is here." There is no longer any need to search for signs of the End, either in heaven or on earth. One has only to look at Jesus' actions and to listen to his preaching. Jesus' ministry is a call for an existential decision, a radical *yes* to God and to a new life. This means a life of love that is to be put into practice in concrete interaction with one's neighbors. The direct encounter with God, brought near to us in the message of Jesus, leads to a direct encounter with our fellow human beings. Jesus brings out what is essential for human existence. We are not asked to subscribe to certain ideas and concepts about God's dealings in the past or in the future, let alone to accept certain apocalyptic constructs. Nor do we receive a set of detailed ethical rules, to be followed in clearly delineated circumstances. Rather, God's offer and claim come to us as a challenge that calls us to respond in faith.

According to Bultmann, Jesus did not claim any messianic designation for himself. And even if he had, it would have no direct impact on our faith. When early Christians, convinced that Jesus had risen from the dead, started to call him "Messiah," "Son of man," "Son of God," and the like, they were giving explicit expression to their belief in the decisive importance of Jesus' ministry. With regard to Jesus himself, Bultmann does not want to go any farther than saying that his call for a decision *implied* a Christology—not in the sense of speculation about a figure coming from heaven or the construction of a particular messianic consciousness, but as an expression of response to God's presence revealed in Jesus' ministry.

All that matters in eschatological statements, by Jesus and by the early Christians, is that they are definitive appeals, made once and for all, to enter into a new existence that is granted to those persons who give up their old selfhood and open themselves to God's grace. Those statements, including their messianic designations and imagery, need to be demythologized—that is, rephrased in nonmythological language. Demythologizing, by doing away with the conceptual trappings that prevent a person from coming to the right decision, will lead to existential interpretation and so to a true self-understanding. In his Shaffer Lectures for 1951 published under the title *Jesus Christ and Mythology*[3] Bultmann made it very clear that demythologizing is not a negative concept, but rather a necessary and positive step toward a better comprehension of the nature of God's relationship with humanity. At the end of this little book he describes his undertaking as an extension in the domain of knowledge and thinking of Paul's and Luther's "justification by faith alone."

## THE SO-CALLED NEW QUEST OF
## THE HISTORICAL JESUS

It was not until 1954 that Bultmann's presuppositions were questioned by one of his own pupils, E. Käsemann. His article "The Problem of the Historical Jesus" was one of the first in a flood of publications on the subject by authors both within and without the school of Bultmann. As has already been remarked in the previous chapter, it is generally regarded as the starting point of the "new quest of the historical Jesus." James M. Robinson's book with the same title appeared in 1959 and was extensively revised for the second German edition,[4] incorporating the continuing debate, partly also provoked by Robinson's own assessment of the prevalent trends in it. As W. G. Kümmel's extensive reports on the *Leben-Jesu-Forschung* in the *Theologische Rundschau*[5] show, the debate by no means slackened or weakened after 1967. Gradually, however, the typical pro- and contra-Bultmannian arguments in the discussion became less prominent.

The problem of the so-called new quest in the school of Bultmann was not so much historical as theological. Bultmann's pupils were engaged in a hermeneutical discussion with their master, among themselves, and with others. The question of the relationship between kerygma and history is at the center of the argument. This is abundantly evident in both versions of J. M. Robinson's assessment of what was going on, and is brought out very clearly in L. E. Keck's *A Future for the Historical Jesus* (1971).[6]

We need not review the debate in question here. The essential points came to the fore in Bultmann's reply to his colleagues in a lecture for the Heidelberg Academy of Sciences in 1960, published two years later.[7] The old master sticks to his guns, at the same time bringing out again what first motivated his radical stand. Of course, he says, the early Christian kerygma speaks about the man Jesus and about no one else. But this does not imply that the kerygmatic Christ is identical with the historical Jesus. The mere fact that the man Jesus existed is sufficient for the proclamation concerning Jesus; in Bultmann's characteristic German, "Das Entscheidende ist schlechthin das Dass" (What is decisive is simply the 'that'; p. 9). Of course historical criticism can establish certain facts about the historical Jesus, but it does not allow us to say anything about Jesus' understanding of his own death. We cannot go beyond the fact of the cross—the cross which is essential for the Christian kerygma concerning the Christ who died for us. It would, in any case, be a perversion of the truth of the kerygma to try to legitimate it by historical facts.

But had Bultmann himself not said that Jesus' entire appearance, and certainly his preaching, does imply a Christology? Bultmann admits that he said as much. Jesus called for a decision for or against himself as messenger of the Word of God, a decision concerned with life and death. Jesus came with authority, as an eschatological figure. This implies a Christology later to be made explicit in the kerygma. It is in fact quite understandable that the proclaimer became the one who was proclaimed. But does all this really matter? After going part of the way with his pupils Bultmann comes to a standstill. It is the kerygma that is truly important, he concludes, and this is not concerned with the preaching of the historical Jesus: it puts itself in the place of all that came before.

Bultmann's pupils, however, continued where their teacher left off. Käsemann,[8] for example, stressed that the search for the historical Jesus seeks to establish the continuity of the one Gospel in the discontinuity of the times and the variety within the kerygma. However much they wanted to convey the message of the present living Lord and were interested in its ethical application, the authors of the gospels and their predecessors told stories about the earthly Jesus and transmitted his sayings. For them, the real turning point in history was not the resurrection but the appearance of Jesus himself, authoritatively confronting humanity with the nearness of the living God. In the much-read *Jesus von Nazareth* (1956)[9] (comparable to Bultmann's *Jesus* written thirty years earlier), G. Bornkamm agrees that the gospels were written in the conviction that the Jesus Christ in whom their authors believed and whom they trusted was the same as the earthly Jesus. Faith does not begin with itself; it is not allowed to indulge in a glorious present but is oriented toward a story of events in the past, a story that has to be told because Christian believers are called upon to follow a master whose life ended on the cross. Jesus did not "preach himself" in the sense of claiming a *Hoheitstitel* for himself. He aroused messianic hopes that he could not fulfill; contrary to the expectations and imaginations of his followers, he died on cross. Jesus preached the coming of the Kingdom of God. Bornkamm's fourth chapter, the first on the teaching of Jesus, begins by quoting Mark 1:14–15: God's Kingdom is there and it is coming. Bornkamm does not deny the future aspects—in fact, he thinks that Jesus reckoned with the immediate arrival of the eschaton (or End)—but he emphasizes the offer of salvation now and the appeal for a decision. It is a decision vis-à-vis the person who comes once and for all with this message of life and death. Jesus went to Jerusalem to preach the message of the Kingdom in the city of the King. He reckoned with opposition and was prepared to face death. This much is historically certain, however uncertain the actual course of events, handed down to us in a tradition shaped by the kerygma, may be in detail.

It is worth noting that Bornkamm shares his teacher's aversion to apocalyptic notions, which both regarded as mistaken attempts to objectify and historicize God's dealings with human beings; like Käsemann and many others both within and without the Bultmann school, he denied that Jesus applied any "messianic titles" to himself. Jesus is unique, not only in the sense that there has never been nor ever will be anyone like him, but also in that he claimed to come with God's definitive offer and appeal. Making God present among men, he could not be enclosed in human words which would try to fix what cannot possibly be fixed. Yet Bultmann was not at all happy with Bornkamm's remark on Jesus' attitude toward his death. Even if the traditional picture and interpretation of Jesus' suffering and death could be proven historically correct, what would we have gained, he asks? Can a historical truth ever legitimate the kerygma?[10]

Repeatedly Ernst Fuchs has emphasized that Jesus' preaching can never be separated from his actions. "From this it follows that Jesus' conduct was itself the real framework of his proclamation."[11] Luke 15 has Jesus tell the parables of the lost sheep and the lost coin and that of the prodigal son in the context of his receiving tax collectors and sinners and eating with them, and rightly so. And if Jesus calls upon his pupils to give up their lives for God's sake, he himself must have been prepared to suffer and die. "From the outset Jesus' relationship to God presupposes suffering." This complete trust in God includes the certainty that God will not allow those who trust him completely (neither Jesus *nor* his followers) to be lost. Small wonder that the gospels not only explain Jesus' suffering and death but also include the message of his resurrection. In doing so they make Jesus' relationship to God explicit.

Again Bultmann disagrees; what should have remained existential interpretation has, in Fuch's hands, become an effort to give historical-psychological explanations.[12] He levels the same objection against Gerhard Ebeling, who characterizes the transition from the proclaimer to the one who was proclaimed as that from the "Witness of Faith" to the "Ground of Faith" and maintains that the second presupposes the first.[13] Of course, Ebeling says, we can never go back beyond the kerygma to prove its legitimacy, but it is nevertheless necessary to ask back (*zurückfragen*) in order to interpret it correctly. The kerygma makes claims about a historical person; Jesus is not a mythical person or a mere "cipher." Only because they refer to Jesus do the words of the kerygma receive a certain meaning. And in its great variety of kerygmatic statements early Christianity orients itself toward Jesus. Unless we assume that this was done completely arbitrarily, we shall have to take seriously that the aim was to make explicit what was implied in Jesus' appearance and in his preaching.

From this rather brief survey it has become clear that Bultmann insisted that the kerygma about Jesus Christ could not and cannot be legitimated by historical facts. In matters of faith, historical-psychological explanations are not valid. His pupils agreed with him to an extent, but they replied that we have to assume a certain measure of continuity between the early Christian preaching about Jesus and Jesus' own words and actions. The early Christian kerygma was concerned with Jesus, a man of flesh and blood whose sayings could be handed down and about whom stories could be told. His life was the framework of his words; he faced death when he decided to go to Jerusalem, and Fuchs even thinks that his readiness to suffer implies his certainty of not being left alone by God. Jesus' post-resurrection followers naturally "asked back" to Jesus and all he stood for. For this reason the quest for the historical Jesus is a necessary and meaningful undertaking for modern Christians. Bultmann's pupils took this seriously, however true to their teacher they remained in their use of existentialist terminology, their aversion to mythological language, and their denial that Jesus claimed any "messianic" titles for himself.

## THE "NEW QUEST" AND BEYOND

Looking back on the turbulent period of the beginning of the "new quest" in the fifties and early sixties, we may wonder whether too much time was devoted to issues that should long have been obvious, and we may ask whether the clash of opinions within and without the Bultmann school always resulted in the discovery of a new truth. We have since moved into the post-Bultmannian era, just as we are now living in the period after Barth and Barthianism. Yet at the time when the debate was taking place, the questions concerned were real issues— for ordinary Christian believers as well as for historians, exegetes, and theologians. The beginning of the new quest took place in a period of transition—especially in Western Europe, which was just recovering from the wounds of World War II and emerging from the hardships after the war. I vividly remember the keen interest shown by active church members in my own country, who, though not theologians, participated in the debate—particularly after a number of issues had been popularized by J. A. T. Robinson in his *Honest to God*.[14] It was generally felt that this was a discussion on the fundamentals of the Christian faith.

People belonging to the post-war generation, including myself, have had to wrestle with the problems raised by Karl Barth and Rudolf Bultmann, and have been attracted and inspired as well as put off by their solutions. Today it is part of our past, a part that has contributed much to our present approach to matters historical and theological, just as the sober and commonsense scholarship of T. W. Manson and other British scholars of his time remains of great value.

For an assessment of Bultmann's theological position, the comments of two scholars may be helpful. First, I would like to point to the section "The Theological Problem" in N. A. Dahl's essay "The Problem of the Historical Jesus," referred to in the previous section. Contrary to other exegetes,[15] Dahl acknowledges Bultmann's position; he had, after all, studied with Bultmann in 1936 and was to publish a thorough review of his *Theology of the New Testament* in 1954.

Faith, Dahl says, is *relatively* uninterested in research on the historical Jesus. This research may, for instance, investigate the events leading up to Jesus' death and the circumstances of the crucifixion, but it can never demonstrate what is crucial to faith and to the church—namely, that Jesus "died for us." Jesus' resurrection cannot be made the object of historical research at all, but for faith Jesus' life and death have their significance in and with the message that God raised him from the dead.

Yet faith is not *absolutely* uninterested in the results of the quest for the historical Jesus. It makes clear that Jesus was a true man with human individuality, and that he belonged to a particular time and a particular milieu. The evangelists were interested "in preserving reliable information concerning what the Lord and Savior did at the time of his earthly life and how his life took shape" (pp. 79–80), and "in all philosophical naïveté it may be regarded as natural and normal that even the present-day believer shares the interest of the evangelists. . . . Existentialist interpretation carried out consistently signifies . . . not only a demythologizing but also a dehistoricizing of the New Testament" (p. 79).

When Bultmann declares the *how* and *what* of the life of Jesus to be theologically irrelevant, "the incarnation of the Word threatens to become a paradox devoid of content" (p. 80). A dehistoricizing approach fails to do justice to the fact that he was so thoroughly human that many people, unable to perceive the hidden glory which others were allowed to see, took offense at him. Early Christians recognized that a radical discontinuity between the Christ of their faith and the man Jesus would be fatal to their kerygma. This is also why the modern quest for the historical Jesus is of theological importance. On the one hand, it would be theologically disastrous if it could be demonstrated that the "real" Jesus was quite different from what the early church claimed him to be. On the other hand, we must concern ourselves with the man Jesus and his message in order to make it clear that he was already in existence before and independent of the proclamation of the church. "He may neither be absorbed by the existential here and now of the kerygma nor by the tradition and the church" (p. 85).

Dahl's response to Bultmann's approach (voiced in its original form, before the discussion in the school of Bultmann had started) is to the point. He correctly stresses that we cannot do justice to the teaching of the early church unless we acknowledge the intrinsic continuity between its kerygma and the ministry of Jesus himself, his word as well as his actions. Dahl demonstrates clearly that modern preoccupations—

however understandable they may be—influence (and hinder) us in our historical approach to early Christianity and to its founder. In saying this, we should, of course, not forget that theological awareness remains a necessary component of historical investigations into the origins of Christianity—not only because we are dealing with events crucial for the faith of a great many present-day believers, but also because the theological claims inherent in the sources need to be studied.

In conclusion, I should like to draw attention to some interesting and helpful comments by Amos N. Wilder on Bultmann's program of demythologizing, found in *The Language of the Gospel: Early Christian Rhetoric.*[16] For Bultmann, myth expresses a specific understanding of human existence, an understanding of human beings as dependent upon powers beyond human control. But it speaks about these powers in inadequate and unsatisfactory ways. It tries to locate them in certain happenings—in the past, the present, or the future—that do not fit into the normal course of events or in certain places—heaven or hell, for instance. For Bultmann this means that mythology tries to pin down, to objectify what is and should remain transcendent. It is a manner of thinking and speaking that conceals rather than conveys what is essential. Demythologizing as existential interpretation brings out what is really intended; it reveals the understanding of human existence that the particular myth seeks to express. For people in the twentieth century there is no access to the heart of the matter, to a new self-understanding (identical with a new understanding of God), without a demythologizing interpretation of the early Christian kerygma.

Amos Wilder goes only part of the way with Bultmann:

> When demythologizing is directed against literalism or against dogmatic objectifying and secularizing of Christian faith and its images, we cannot but approve its aim. Faith should not be acceptance of pictures of God's dealings taken as blueprints for belief, let alone credulity,

he says. But he immediately adds:

> Demythologizing fails to do justice to the meaning of truth in the imagery. In waiving the wisdom of the myth for a supposed more fundamental meaning in terms of encounter, it seems motivated

by a radical despair with respect to the possibilities of human knowing. In this scepticism all that understanding of the world and of the course in the world and of history which is imaged forth in the Christian revelation is surrendered as though of the order of fiction, and, indeed, as if it were a dangerous ideology. (pp. 133–134)

Wilder emphasizes that early Christian language was dynamic and imaginative; of necessity it created myths to give expression to an awareness of having been granted a new existence, of living at the threshold of a new era, of receiving new energy through the Spirit of God. Old images, of which the scriptures of Israel were replete, were revived, and new images were created. Early Christians understood themselves as living in a new relationship to God, and they expressed this new experience in new myths. These myths sought not only to convey truth about man (and woman) but also to clarify God's relationship to history, to the past and the future of the whole of humanity—in fact, to God's entire creation.

Wilder is right in suggesting that dynamic speech creates images and myths, and that the meaning of myth cannot be confined to a form of human self-understanding. This means that caution is in order as we analyze the terms, concepts, and images present in sayings handed down as words of Jesus or in early Christian teaching about Jesus. We shall have to study them in the historical context in which they occurred, as verbal expressions of a particular life-experience of people raised in the ancient traditions of Israel and living around the eastern part of the Mediterranean in the Roman Empire.

We shall have to take very seriously the fact that Jesus was a Jew and that early Christianity started as a movement within Judaism. Prophetic words, parables, wisdom-sayings, apocalyptic imagery, and the like will have to be explained against the background of Israel's scriptures, which were regarded as authoritative but explained in many different ways by Jews (and their sympathizers) of various persuasions—including the followers of Jesus. In order to discover what is traditional and what is new (and how the new can be understood against the backdrop of the traditional), in order to detect that which seemed conventional yet has taken on a new meaning in a new context, careful tradition criticism

and comparative study of religious concepts and ideas are indispens-
able.[17] We must be careful not to modernize Jesus or his early followers
but should try to understand them as children of a particular country at
a particular time, using a language of their own in speaking about God,
humanity, and the world.

# III

## *Jesus'*
## *Mission*
## *and His Death*
## *on the Cross*

Jesus' life ended on the cross, a fact of crucial importance for early and present-day Christians alike. The value and significance of the crucifixion are inextricably bound up with Jesus' person, with his intentions and his own understanding of his death as the consummation of his mission. Had Jesus not stood in a unique relationship with God and had he not been fully aware of everything this involved, the crucifixion would have been robbed of its dignity and its depth of meaning. It would have been merely a wanton (if legal) execution of one out of many—an event, for that matter, hardly likely to be recorded in history. It would have been a fate suffered by one individual, devoid of greater implications. But since it concerned Jesus, it was not a case of "his not to reason why, his but to do and die." In other words, without Jesus' active participation in the events leading up to a death that he accepted of his own free will for the sake of others, this death could never have become the supreme sacrifice that it is within Christianity's scheme of reference. Following the inner logic of Jesus' entire mission, it formed its apogee in the purest sense of the word.

For that reason I shall attempt in this chapter to determine what can be known about Jesus' own attitude toward his death. Did he foresee it? Did he even seek it out? What meaning did he attach to it in view of the mission entrusted to him by God?

In line with the arguments developed in the preceding chapters, I shall take as my starting point the various interpretations of Jesus' death found in the oldest strata of traditional Christian material. Only in the second instance shall I take into account a number of sayings of Jesus recorded in the synoptic gospels and try to determine to what extent they convey or reflect what Jesus thought and said and how they fit into the context of what is reported about his actions.[1]

The traditional expressions and patterns of thought stem from the communities of the earliest followers of Jesus after his death. This death, a shattering event, had to be explained. Its meaning had to be understood both in the context of Jesus' own mission and in view of their conviction that this mission was now being continued, thanks to Jesus' victory over death. Jesus' followers believed in a living Lord who guided their lives through the Spirit and who would return in order to realize the sovereign rule of God on earth, which he had announced and inaugurated during his mission in Galilee and Judea.

In their attempts to grasp the meaning of Jesus' death, his followers were led by their conviction that Jesus had indeed been sent by God at a crucial moment in history and that God had vindicated him. He had died on the cross, but he was no criminal or revolutionary, much less a pious man or a prophet who, in the eyes of his executioners, had deluded his followers and himself. Not only was the message of Jesus' death on the cross, in the words of Paul, a "stumbling block to Jews and folly to Gentiles" (1 Cor. 1:23), an impediment to hostile opponents and interested outsiders alike; even for those who firmly believed in the continuing leadership of their living master, his death required clarification. Meditating on the divine "necessity" of Jesus' death (Mark 8:31) and combing the scriptures (see, e.g., 1 Cor. 15:3–4 with the phrase "in accordance with the scriptures" and Mark 14:21), they searched for other examples of servants of God who had suffered and died and had been vindicated. What had been taught about them was used to explain what had happened to Jesus.

From the very beginning, various models of interpretation were applied, and as Christian reflection continued, the variety became even greater. For our present purposes I shall concentrate on three conceptions found in traditional material incorporated in Paul, Q, and Mark: (*a*) the interpretation of Jesus' death as that of an envoy of God rejected by Israel; (*b*) the conception of Jesus as a suffering, righteous servant of God; and (*c*) the view of Jesus' death as a death for others.[2]

These models of interpretation are not mutually exclusive but complementary, if only because they aim at elucidating essential aspects of
the life and death (and continuing activity) of one person, Jesus. We
shall find, however, that these approaches cannot, either individually or
taken together, explain everything about Jesus. Jesus is not just any
messenger sent by God, but the ultimate envoy; he is not just any
suffering, righteous servant of God, but servant and Son of God par
excellence. In one type of formula for speaking about Jesus' death for
others, we find *Christos* as subject: "*Christ* died for us (you)." The use of
this designation for Jesus is one indication that with his death (and
resurrection) a definitive turning point has been reached, a new era has
begun. Along with all the discontinuity, which should be neither denied
nor belittled, there is also continuity between the Christian kerygma
after Easter and Jesus' announcement and inauguration of God's Kingdom before Easter, which includes the call for a decision concerning his
own person.

Only in the next chapter will this continuity receive full treatment,
but we shall have to begin to ask here in what respects the interpretations given after Easter presuppose the views on Jesus' life and death
held by his followers even before his death on the cross. In doing so, we
cannot exclude the possibility, of course, that cautious but persistent
"asking back" will lead us to aspects of Jesus' *own* interpretation of his
life and death in faithful obedience to God—however difficult (or even,
in the end, impossible) it may be to reconstruct the precise words
spoken by Jesus and to determine his exact actions.

## JESUS AS AN ENVOY OF GOD
## REJECTED BY ISRAEL

In Paul's first letter to the Thessalonians we find a bitter
reproach by the Jew Paul of those Jews who "killed both the Lord Jesus
and the prophets, and drove us out, and displease God and oppose all
men by hindering us from speaking to the Gentiles that they may be
saved—so as always to fill up the measure of their sins. But God's wrath
has come upon them for ever." (2:15–16, RSV margin). In this passage, a
small digression in the letter, Paul draws on traditional material[3] to link

the killing of Jesus, who is named first and is expressly called "the Lord," with the killing of the prophets and the persecution of Jesus' followers. He emphasizes that the iniquity of the Jews is now complete. The limit has been reached; the hour of judgment has arrived.

A similar view is found in the Q-passage Luke 11:49–51 (par. Matt. 23:34–36). In Luke's version, very likely representing that of Q, we read: "Therefore also the Wisdom of God said, 'I will send them prophets and apostles, some of whom they will kill and persecute,' that the blood of all the prophets, shed from the foundation of the world, may be required of this generation.... Yes, I tell you, it shall be required of this generation." Again it is stressed that the climax has been reached, that judgment and punishment are at hand. Among the prophets and envoys sent by Wisdom are John the Baptist and Jesus, who in the Q-passage Luke 7:31–35 (par. Matt. 11:16–19) are called "the children of Wisdom"—both rejected by "this generation," though for different reasons. Of course, Christian messengers after Jesus are also included. Matthew, who has Jesus himself announce the persecution, mentions only prophets and wise men sent by Jesus. The announcement is found in Luke and in Matthew in the context of a whole series of accusations against the Pharisees and the scribes or lawyers. Matthew adds the well-known saying, "O Jerusalem, Jerusalem, killing the prophets and stoning those who are sent to you!" (23:37, identical with Luke 13:34, though placed in a different context there). Mark offers the parable of the vineyard, in which the son of the vineyard's owner is killed as his father's final envoy after a number of messengers have been beaten, wounded, and killed (Mark 12:1–9). The son stands for Jesus, the other messengers for the prophets. Again, God's intervention is said to be at hand. The owner of the vineyard "will come and destroy the tenants, and give the vineyard to others" (v. 9).

This theme, then, is found in Pauline material, in Q, and in Mark. We may add Luke 6:22–23 (par. Matt. 5:11–12)—a Q-passage in which the persecution of Jesus' followers is compared to that of the prophets earlier in history—and Acts 7:51–53—where Stephen, about to be martyred himself, accuses the Jews of persecuting the prophets and betraying and murdering him whose coming they announced. As O. H. Steck has shown,[4] these early Christian statements fit into a series of passages found in the Old Testament and other ancient Jewish writings that criticize Israel's rejection of the prophets who are sent again and again to bring Israel back to a life of obedience to God.

This line of interpretation was clearly popular among early Christians; it explained not only the death of Jesus but also the sufferings and persecutions they themselves were subjected to by the Jewish authorities. Israel had acted like this all the time! Only *now* the measure of sins was full; with the killing of God's final envoy, Jesus, the decisive turning point had come.

Interestingly, this model of interpretation (which emphasizes the negative response of the persecutors rather than the obedience and faithfulness of the messengers) does not speak of Jesus' resurrection as his vindication. After the parable in 12:1–9, to be sure, Mark adds a reference to the resurrection by quoting Ps. 118:22–23, and Acts 7:51–53 is followed in verse 55 by a vision of Jesus standing at the right hand of God in heaven.[5] But the basic pattern implies the vindication of Jesus, his followers, and all preceding messengers at the impending judgment on Israel. Strikingly, also no positive meaning is attached to Jesus' death or to that of others.

Those who handed down words of Jesus like the ones from Q and Mark just cited did so because of the connection and continuity they saw between themselves and the disciples who had followed Jesus during his lifetime and had been sent out on incidental missions by Jesus himself. Then and now, solidarity between pupil and master, envoy and sender counted.

We are not in a position to determine exactly the authentic kernel in the words on discipleship found in Mark and Q. But if we compare, for example, Mark 8:34–9:1 (par.) and 10:17–31 (par.)[6] with Luke 14:26–27 (par. Matt. 10:37–38) and Luke 9:57–62 (par. Matt. 8:18–22), or if we read Mark's account of the commissioning of the Twelve in 6:6b–13 beside the corresponding Q-pericope in Luke 10:2–12 (par. Matt. 9:37–38; 10:16, 9–13, 7–8a, 14–15), we find many converging statements.

Preaching and healing in the name of their master, the disciples will meet with the opposition and rejection he himself had to face. Mark places the commissioning of the Twelve appositely after the story of Jesus' rejection at Nazareth, an illustration of the truth of the proverb "a prophet is not without honor, except in his own country, and among his own kin, and in his own house" (Mark 6:4). It is followed by the story of the killing of John the Baptist by Herod Antipas (6:17–29).

Q has preserved the condemnation of the Galilean cities of Chorazin, Bethsaida, and Capernaum (Luke 10:13–15, par. Matt. 11:20–24). In the final judgment it will be more tolerable for Tyre and Sidon than for the inhabitants of these three cities, because they did not repent after the mighty works done in them—by Jesus himself, according to Matthew, or by Jesus' disciples, according to Luke, who connects this passage with that of the commissioning of the Seventy. Another Q-passage, Luke 11:29–30 (par. Matt. 12:38–42), compares the reaction of the present evil generation unfavorably with the response of Nineveh to Jonah and of the Queen of the South to Solomon. The Ninevites "repented at the preaching of Jonah, and behold, something greater than Jonah is here" (v. 32), just as "something greater than Solomon is here" (v. 31).

Jesus was met with unbelief and rejection, as were his disciples. John the Baptist, another messenger of God who came immediately before Jesus and was directly linked with him, had been murdered. It is extremely likely that not only Jesus' followers but also Jesus himself viewed John's fate, the opposition they faced, and the possibility of violent death for themselves, in the light of those passages from Scripture that denounced Israel's violent rejection of messengers sent by God.

### JESUS AS A SUFFERING RIGHTEOUS SERVANT

In Luke 6:22–23 (par. Matt. 5:11–12) the exclusion and reviling of Jesus' followers on account of the Son of man ("on my account," Matt. 5:11) is compared with the persecution of the prophets by their (the Jews') fathers. Yet this suffering is also a reason for joy: "Your reward is great in heaven." Those who suffer hardship because of Jesus are blessed, just as those who are poor shall receive the Kingdom of God, those that hunger now shall be satisfied, and those that weep now shall laugh (Luke 6:20–21 par. Matt. 5:3, 6, [4]). The series of four beatitudes found in Luke very likely marked the beginning of Jesus' teaching in Q. When the Kingdom of God, now breaking forth on earth, becomes full reality, then poverty, hunger, and sorrow will vanish and those who remain faithful to the one who has inaugurated this Kingdom will be rewarded by God. Mark 13:9–13 (and par.), depicting the troubles that lie ahead for those who wish to remain loyal to the message of the Gospel, ends with the assurance, "But he who endures to the end will be saved" (see also Matt. 10:22). Similarly, in the section on the consequences of discipleship in Mark 8:34–9:1 (and par.) we find the promise that "whoever loses his life for my sake and the gospel's will save it" (v. 35, par. Matt. 16:25; Luke 9:24; John 12:25 and Matt. 10:39, par. Luke 17:33 [Q]). That person will have a share in the Kingdom of God when it reveals itself in power, inaugurated by the Son of man coming "in the glory of his Father with the holy angels" (8:38; 9:1 and par.).

According to these words of Jesus found in Mark and Q, those who follow Jesus, bringing his message and serving his cause until the very end, will be vindicated. They may expect to suffer and must be ready to give their lives, but they may also expect to share in the blessings of God's Kingdom, due to be revealed in the near future.

Mark connects the announcement of the sufferings and vindication of the disciples with the first of three predictions of Jesus' passion and resurrection "after three days" that figure prominently in his gospel (8:31; 9:31; 10:32–33). After all, Jesus' disciples are called upon to come *after him*. It is clear that the first and, even more so, the third of these predictions have been modeled on the events recorded later in the gospel. But it has often been argued that the short prediction in 9:31— "The Son of man will be delivered into the hands of men, and they will kill him; and when he is killed, after three days he will rise"—may, in its essence, go back to Jesus himself. This seems likely, though we shall never be able to prove it conclusively. As C. K. Barrett has said, "If . . . Jesus did (in forms not fully recoverable) predict and interpret his approaching passion, the interpretation must have included the predic- tion of some kind of vindication beyond the passion. It is inconceivable that Jesus simply predicted the complete and final failure of his mis- sion."[7] He regards it as possible that the words "after three days he will rise," which in their *present* context point forward to Mark 16:1–8 (cf. the ancient formula from 1 Cor. 15:3–5, with the phrase "he was raised on the third day"), originally indicated Jesus' exaltation and vindication a short time after his violent death. Barrett has drawn attention to Mark 14:25: "Truly, I say to you, I shall not drink again of the fruit of the vine until that day when I drink it new in the kingdom of God" (cf. Luke 22:15–19). These words, spoken at the Last Supper Jesus shares with his disciples, look beyond the imminent passion to Jesus' participation in the joys of the fully realized Kingdom.

In support of the thesis that Jesus himself may have been convinced that his passion would be followed by his vindication, we may point to the rich and variegated tradition found in the Old Testament and other early Jewish literature of God's rescuing his faithful servants who, though in distress, poverty, or oppression, continue to place their trust in him. Jesus is portrayed as a faithful and obedient servant of God, living in close communion with God, whom, according to Q, he addressed as Father (see Luke 10:21–23, par. Matt. 11:25–27; 11:2, par. Matt. 6:9; Mark 14:36 and par.; further substantiated by Gal. 4:6 and Rom. 8:15). Jesus is shown as placing his trust in God's power to deliver him and all the faithful.

The theme of God's righteous suffering servant recurs in numerous passages and with many variations in form and content.[8] The vital connection between these servants' complete trust in God and his deliverance of them, reiterated throughout these passages, is expressed in Psalm 34:17–19 with the words:

> When the righteous cry for help, the LORD hears,
> and delivers them out of their troubles.
> The LORD is near to the brokenhearted,
> and saves the crushed in spirit.
> Many are the afflictions of the righteous;
> but the LORD delivers him out of them all.

God often helps the afflicted by bringing a radical turn in their lives—as, for example, in a number of psalms (that consequently combine lament and prayer with thanksgiving) and in the stories of the three young men in the fiery furnace in Daniel 3 and of Daniel himself in the lions' den in Daniel 6. In Daniel 3 and 6, God's faithful servants are prepared to give their lives for God's sake, but at the crucial moment an angel sent by God comes to their rescue. God faithfully delivered his servants "who trusted in him . . . and yielded up their bodies rather than serve and worship any god except their own God" (Dan. 3:28; cf. 6:20–22, 25–27).

Some texts, many of them apocalyptic ones, go a decisive step further by connecting God's vindication of his faithful servants with his final intervention in the affairs of the world, and by introducing the idea of resurrection. This is the case in Dan. 11:29–35 and 12:1–3; 1 Enoch 102–104, Syr. Bar. 48:48–50 and 52:6–7, and in the texts from Q and Mark mentioned above. Special mention should be made of two passages from the Wisdom of Solomon, 2:12–20 and 5:1–7. In the first of these two passages a righteous man who professes to have knowledge of God, calls himself "servant of God," and knows that God is his father (vv. 13, 16) is condemned to death by his opponents. "Let us see if his words are true, and let us test what will happen at the end of his life, for if the righteous man is God's son, he will help him" (vv. 17–18). God does help him; in 5:1–7 it is his opponents who stand condemned. They have no choice but to confess that he has truly served God. He is "numbered among the sons of God" and "his lot is among the saints" (v. 5). The wicked are dispersed like chaff or smoke before the wind, but the righteous live forever (vv. 15–16). Although, as George Nickelsburg has argued, "the eschatological time-table of Wisdom is far from clear,"[9] these passages seem to suggest that the righteous who are persecuted will be exalted and vindicated straight away, and that their persecutors will have to witness their glory and acknowledge their own guilt after their victims' death before they themselves are destroyed altogether. Whatever the exact timetable, the important point is that God is righteous and faithful to those who obey him completely and place their trust in him.

In the Markan passion story the words "My God, my God, why hast thou forsaken me" from Psalm 22, one of the psalms of the suffering righteous, are Jesus' last understandable utterance before his death (Mark 15:34; Matt. 27:46). These words are even given in Aramaic before being translated into Greek. Scholars have collected other references, both explicit and implicit, to passages representing the various aspects of the tradition of the suffering righteous, and it is quite possible that even at an earlier stage they helped mold the story of Jesus' passion on the cross.[10] The use of Ps. 22:1 is intended to suggest the expectation of divine deliverance, I think. Luke, clearly wanting to avoid misunderstanding, replaced the quotation from Ps. 22:1 by a phrase taken from another psalm of suffering and deliverance, "Into thy hand I commit my spirit" (Ps. 31:5). Later on in the story God's vindication of his suffering servant Jesus is expressed in terms of resurrection and exaltation. In Mark 16:6 the young man in a white robe sitting inside the empty tomb announces to the women that the crucified Jesus has been raised; his disciples will see him in Galilee. And at the trial before the Sanhedrin, just before his condemnation by Pilate and his crucifixion, Jesus declares openly that he is "the Christ, the Son of the Blessed" and that those who are about to condemn him "will see the Son of man sitting at the right hand of Power, and coming with the clouds of heaven" (14:61–62).

This scene is reminiscent of that pictured in Wisd. Sol. 2:12–20 and 5:1–7, as is the scene of mockery in 15:29–32. The connection is brought out even more clearly in the parallel passage in Matt. 27:38–43, which has the additional words, "He trusts in God; let God deliver him now, if he desires him; for he said, 'I am the Son of God.'" In Mark 15:39 the Roman centurion at the cross declares: "Truly this man was a son of God!"

For Mark (and the other evangelists) Jesus is not just any servant, any son of God; he is "the Christ, *the* Son of the Blessed" (14:61). Jesus' solemn declaration, "I am; and you will see the Son of man sitting at the right hand of Power, and coming with the clouds of heaven" (v. 62) marks a significant turning point in Mark's story. Here Jesus says openly to his opponents (and indirectly to the readers of the Gospel) who he is. As George Nickelsburg has said, the use of the genre of the story of the righteous one in the passion narrative served "to describe how the death and exaltation of Jesus brought the old order to an end."[11] It is clear that the convictions and beliefs of the early Christians in the period after Jesus' death have exercised a considerable influence on the transmission of the stories brought together in Mark 14–16. Referring back to my discussion in chapter 1 of T. W. Manson's reliance on the Markan framework, I consider it wise not to base a reconstruction of what factually happened, and of what historically motivated Jesus and his closest followers, on this narrative.

If we wish to maintain that Jesus, in all likelihood, expected not only to suffer and to die but also to be vindicated by God, we must nonetheless be cautious about using the argument that he must have been acquainted with the tradition of God's help for his suffering servants (in its many forms). We should note, however, that his announcement of the coming of God's sovereign rule on earth implied the expectation that it would soon be completely realized, and that this, in turn, would bring the vindication of the one who inaugurated it *and* of those who had been sent out by him to preach, exorcise, and heal in his name. Jesus' frequent use of the term "Son of man," in Mark as well as in Q, may also point in that direction. After all, in Daniel 7 the "one like a son of man" who stands for the saints of the Most High, oppressed by "the little horn" of the fourth beast (vv. 21, 25), receives an everlasting Kingdom.

## JESUS AS THE MAN WHO DIED FOR OTHERS

The notion that Jesus died for others—or, more specifically, for the sins of others—is widespread in the oldest stratum of tradition. The longer expression gives an explanation of the shorter one, as Paul makes clear in Rom. 5:1–11, where he emphasizes that "while we were yet helpless, at the right time Christ died for the ungodly" (v. 6) and "while we were yet sinners Christ died for us" (v. 8). These two statements elaborate on the formula "Christ died for us/you" (*Christos apethanen hyper hēmōn/humōn*) found in Rom. 14:15; 1 Cor. 8:11 (with the preposition *dia* instead of *hyper*); 1 Cor. 15:3 ("for our sins"; in the context of a formula dealing with death and resurrection); and 1 Thess. 5:10.[12] It is implied as well in Rom. 14:9; 1 Cor. 1:13; 2 Cor. 5:21; Gal. 2:21, 3:13.[13]

The meaning of the formula is brought out clearly, again by Paul, in 2 Cor. 5:14–15: "For the love of Christ controls us, because we are convinced that one has died for all; therefore all have died. And he died for all, that those who live might live no longer for themselves but for him who for their sake died and was raised." What happened to the "one" happened to the "many." If, then, Christ died for the sake of those connected with him in faith, they too have died and are under the obligation to live a new life for him who was raised to a new life after his death.

In Rom. 6:2–10 and Gal. 3:26–29 this central idea of a close communion between Jesus Christ and those belonging to him is expressed in connection with baptism. In Galatians 3 all believers are said to be children of God "in Christ Jesus"; in being baptized into Christ they have "put on Christ." In Romans 6 this idea of communion is linked with that of Jesus' death and resurrection. Those who "have been baptized into Christ Jesus were baptized into his death" (v. 3). Paul continues: "We were buried therefore with him by baptism into death, so that as Christ was raised from the dead by the glory of the Father, we too might walk in newness of life" (v. 4). This form of corporate thinking constitutes an essential element in Paul's theology but probably goes back to corporate experiences in the context of the baptismal ritual.[14]

The *hyper*-formulas as well as the corporate terminology make it clear that what happens to someone who represents others has a direct impact on those associated with that person. In the case of Jesus Christ, if people have sinned and their relationship with God has been disturbed, then the death of one who has not sinned (as Paul states explicitly in 2 Cor. 5:21) effectively restores this relationship and takes away consequences of sin—for those who put their trust in him and live in communion with him.

In the traditions surrounding the Last Supper the same thought is expressed with the help of covenant terminology. The two oldest versions of that story, those found in Mark 14:22–25 and in 1 Cor. 11:23–26 (clearly handed down in a form to be recited at the commemoration of the Lord's death by Christian communities), are worded somewhat differently from each other but express the same basic idea. Mark 14:24 speaks of "my blood of the covenant, which is poured out for many" (Matt. 26:28 adds "for the forgiveness of sins"). The word "many" used here (and in Mark 10:45), in the context of the Gospel of Mark suggests the spreading of the Gospel message to all nations; in itself it only presupposes the notion of representation also found in 2 Cor. 5:14–15. Paul has "for you" and connects this expression with the bread: "This is my body which is broken for you" (1 Cor. 11:24). In the next verse he speaks of "this cup" as "the new covenant in my blood."

To complement this picture we should look briefly at the so-called surrender formulas in which the verbs *paradidonai* (to give up) and *didonai* (to give) occur. In the opening of his letter to the Galatians Paul speaks about "our Lord Jesus Christ who gave himself for our sins" (vv. 3–4); later in the same letter he professes to live by faith in the Son of God, "who loved me and gave himself for me" (2:20). In Rom. 8:32 the agent behind Jesus' sacrifice is God ("He who did not spare his own Son but gave him up for us all"),[15] and in Rom. 4:24–25 he is the implied subject: "Jesus our Lord . . . was put to death for our trespasses and raised for our justification." Additions to the formula try to make clearer what it wants to convey. Eph. 5:2 (cf. v. 25) says: "Christ loved us and gave himself up for us, a fragrant offering and a sacrifice to God," and in Mark 10:45 we encounter the well-known phrase "the Son of man . . . came not to be served but to serve, and to give his life as a ransom for (*anti*) many" (cf. Matt. 20:28; 1 Tim. 2:6; Tit. 2:14).

Wherever the concept of Jesus' death for others is found, it is spoken of as having brought a definitive change in the relationship between God and those who belong to Jesus. It is not just one particular man called Jesus who died; in one way or another, his special status is always emphasized. In the "died for us/you" formulas the subject is usually Christ, and the connection between death and resurrection is sometimes made explicit; in the surrender formulas the subject is frequently "Son of God" or "Son of man." Jesus' death has a lasting effect. In Rom. 5:1–11, for instance, Paul links reconciliation with God now to salvation from God's eschatological judgment in the future. In Gal. 1:4 he declares that Jesus Christ "gave himself for our sins to deliver us from the present evil age." Communion is celebrated in expectation of the coming of the Kingdom of God. Paul writes, "as you eat this bread and drink the cup, you proclaim the Lord's death until he comes" (1 Cor. 11:26), and, as mentioned previously, Mark includes in his recounting of the Last Supper Jesus' words about drinking the fruit of the vine new in the Kingdom of God (14:25). In short, this interpretation of Jesus' death as the supreme sacrifice on behalf of humankind, to be accepted in faith, is firmly embedded in the Christian view of Jesus' mission as the decisive turning point in God's dealings with Israel and the world.

It is clear that in this pattern of thought Jesus' death cannot be regarded separately from his life. His death could not have served God's purpose had his life not been dedicated to the service of God and humankind all along. When Paul writes, "For our sake he made him to be sin who knew no sin" (2 Cor. 5:21), he expresses what was common conviction. The one who gave his life as a ransom for many came not to be served but to serve (Mark 10:45) The Lukan parallel to this saying, given in the context of Jesus' Last Supper with his disciples (Luke 22:25–27), does not mention Jesus' death as a ransom but ends with the words "I am among you as one who serves" (cf. also John 13:4–17).

The early Christian interpretation of Jesus' death for others may be further elucidated by a comparison with the account of the death of Eleazar and that of the seven brothers and their mother in 2 Macc. 6:18–31 and 2 Macc. 7, and in 4 Macc. 5–7 and 4 Macc. 8–18. These two Hellenistic-Jewish writings, which date from around 124 B.C.E. and from the end of the first century C.E. respectively, were strongly influenced by Greek, Hellenistic, and Roman ideas about dying for one's city or one's friend, for the law or for truth, and also about expiatory sacrifice to assuage the anger of the gods.[16] But that should not lead us to the all-too-simple conclusion that the ideas found there are illustrative only of the background of ideas concerning Jesus' death current in Hellenistic Christianity. In these two writings, Hellenistic conceptions are used to explain the death of martyrs obedient to the God of Israel, and there is no reason to assume a rigid separation between Palestinian and Hellenistic Judaism or between Palestinian and Hellenistic congregations in first-century Christianity.[17]

In 2 and 4 Maccabees the expressions "to die for" and "to give one's life for" are, above all, used in connection with the law. Eleazar is willing to die a good death "for the revered and holy laws" (2 Macc. 6:28), and the seven brothers "give up body and life for the law of our fathers" (2 Macc. 7:37). In 4 Maccabees the martyrs are said to have died "for the law" (6:27; 13:9), "for virtue's sake" (1:8), or "for the sake of reverence for God" (*eusebeia;* 9:6; 18:3). Many related expressions are found; all emphasize the martyrs' true obedience to God's commandments and their readiness to die rather than transgress any of them, even under the greatest pressure on the part of the tyrant.

Yet the martyrs in 2 Maccabees also share in the sins and the punishment of their people (7:18, 32). In 7:33 the last of the seven brothers to be martyred declares: "And if our living God is angry for a little while, to rebuke and discipline us, he will again be reconciled with his own servants." The effect of the death of the martyrs, in solidarity with Israel, is indeed that God is reconciled with his people (1:5; 5:20; 8:29) and that God's wrath turns into mercy. In 8:1–7 this is evident in the victories of Judas Maccabaeus and his army of faithful Jews over the enemy. In his last words the youngest brother prays for Israel, asking God "to show mercy soon to our nation . . . and through me and my brothers to bring to an end the wrath of the Almighty which has justly fallen on our whole nation" (7:37–38).

As for the martyrs themselves, they will be vindicated by God; 2 Maccabees 7 repeatedly stresses their resurrection (vv. 9, 11, 14, 23, 29, 36). A few times a bodily resurrection seems to be envisaged: the martyr expects to recover his tortured limbs through God (v. 9; 14:46) and the mother expects to get her seven sons back in God's mercy (v. 29). But there is also reason to think that, like Onias and Jeremiah in 15:12–16, they will receive some form of existence in heaven (see 7:36). For the tyrant, the antagonist of God and his people, there will be no resurrection to life. He will not escape punishment (vv. 17, 19, 31, 34–37; chapter 9).

The martyrs in 4 Maccabees also receive eternal life after death, together with all God's faithful in the past, martyrs, near-martyrs, and people otherwise in distress, under the leadership of Abraham, Isaac, and Jacob (see, e.g., 7:18–19; 13:17; 18:23–24). The death of the martyrs has a direct impact on the land and the people (18:3–4). In 6:28–29 Eleazar dies, willingly, for the sake of (*dia*) the Law. He prays to God: "Be merciful to your people and let our punishment be a satisfaction on their behalf [here we find *hyper* plus personal pronoun]. Make my blood their purification and take my life as a ransom for theirs."[18] The same idea recurs in 17:21, 22: "and the tyrant was punished and our land purified, since they became, as it were, a ransom for the sins of our nation.[19] Through the blood of these righteous ones and through the propitiation[20] of their death the divine providence rescued Israel, which had been shamefully treated."

In 2 and 4 Maccabees[21] the death of the faithful Israelites brings about a decisive change for Israel. The martyrs themselves are vindicated and exalted to live with God. They act and die as representatives of the people; therefore, Israel will benefit from the supreme loyalty to God that led them to their self-sacrifice.

Neither 2 Maccabees nor 4 Maccabees places this story in an eschatological context. At the end of 4 Maccabees (18:4) the nation lives in peace thanks to the martyrs, who are said to have restored the observance of the law (*eunomia*). The emphasis, however, is on the fate of the martyrs themselves, who have demonstrated that those who obey the law recognize that devout reason is master of the passions—not only of the pains that come from within, but also of those that come from outside ourselves. Those who understood and followed this were deemed worthy of a divine inheritance (18:1–3).

In 2 Maccabees the death of Eleazar and of the seven brothers together with their mother marks a turning point in God's relationship with Israel—and, as a result, also in the military situation of Israel, so that, in the end, the temple is cleansed and temple worship restored. History has a way of repeating itself, however: the last battle mentioned in 2 Maccabees (chapter 15) is won after Razis in 14:37–46 had been martyred.[22]

The analogy between the concept of Jesus' death for others and this view of the martyrs is evident; there are even agreements in terminology (cf., e.g., 2 Macc. 7:33, 37–38 and Rom. 5:6–11). But with Jesus' death the eschatological element comes in. Jesus has, in the eyes of his followers, a special position as inaugurator of a new era in God's dealings with humanity. In his case God's intervention proved not only decisive, but also definitive.[23] This is expressed by those connected with Jesus in terms of forgiveness, reconciliation, redemption, and hope for salvation from the wrath of God's final judgment. Furthermore, it is not restricted to those who belong to Israel and truly obey God's commandments but includes all—Jews and non-Jews—who have placed their trust in Jesus as God's final envoy.

Jesus saw as his mission the inauguration of the definitive change inherent to the coming of God's Kingdom. It is certainly possible and even probable that during his preaching in Galilee and Jerusalem, when his death had become a possibility to be reckoned with very seriously, Jesus, or Jesus' followers, considered this to be the death of a martyr, but decisive proof cannot be given. Whether they thought of his death in terms of the traditional material discussed in this section, we are not in a position to say. Most of what has been handed down about Jesus' own views of his death is found in the letters of Paul; nothing is found in Q (which never speaks explicitly about the meaning of Jesus' death) and only two closely related sayings (10:45 and 14:24) are found in Mark. The second of these is bound up with the early Christian liturgy of the Holy Supper, which may have influenced its transmission. The most we can say is that Jesus, convinced of the speedy and complete realization of God's Kingdom and his own vindication after his death, may have regarded his death as serving God's purpose. In what terms he expressed this, we do not know for certain.[24]

### AN EXCURSUS INTO
### TWO RELATED QUESTIONS

In the attempt to determine Jesus' own attitude toward his death, two questions have received considerable attention and should be assessed briefly here. One involves the possible influence of the Fourth Servant Song in Isa. 52:13–53:12 on early Christian interpretations of the death of Jesus and, according to many, also on Jesus' own view of his impending death. The other is the significance of the term "Son of man."

## The Fourth Servant Song

A few decades ago it had become "almost an axiom of . . . New Testament study that most of the New Testament writers, and probably our Lord himself, were controlled in their Christological thinking by the figure of the Suffering Servant of the Lord."[25] In this respect the work of J. Jeremias was very influential,[26] as was that of O. Cullmann, who devoted a chapter of his *Christology of the New Testament* to "Jesus the Suffering Servant of God."[27] T. W. Manson should be mentioned here as well, because (as I have already noted) he saw a strong connection between the notions Son of man and Servant of the Lord in Jesus' life and thought. Today, however, many scholars are of the opinion that the importance of the idea of the suffering servant for early Christianity has been greatly overrated; moreover, it is difficult to demonstrate that Jesus himself interpreted his destiny in light of this passage from Scripture. This has been shown convincingly by C. K. Barrett in an important contribution to the memorial volume for T. W. Manson[28] and by M. D. Hooker in her *Jesus and the Servant.*
Whoever may be envisaged in the Fourth Servant Song (the righ-

teous in Israel or the prophet, or both), a decisive turn in the fate of God's servant is announced. In 53:1–10 the servant's sufferings unto death are described at great length and interpreted as sufferings on behalf of the sins of others (see vv. 4–6, 10, 12). Interestingly, this interpretation of suffering stands apart in Old Testament literature, and with regard to its influence on later texts M. Hengel has pointed out that "so far . . . we have no clear text from pre-Christian Judaism which speaks of the vicarious suffering of the Messiah in connection with Isa. 53."[29]

This, of course, does not exclude the possibility that early Christians did use this passage. In fact, Hengel (who aims at restoring the balance after recent neglect of Isaiah 53) is firmly convinced that "Isa. 53 had an influence on the origin and shaping of the earliest kerygma." He says: "Neither the formula of the 'surrender' of Jesus nor that of his representative dying 'for many' or 'for us' would have come into being without the background of this mysterious prophecy."[30] The suffering servant of Isa. 50:4–11 and Isa. 52:13–53:12 certainly could provide a suitable model for the explanation of Jesus' life, death, and vindication. The person portrayed here is an ideal servant of the Lord, a prophetic figure speaking on God's behalf against God's and his own adversaries, ready to suffer. This servant resembles the other prophetic envoys rejected by Israel and is one of the suffering righteous ones. He is closely related to those martyrs who refused to buckle under to tyrants and died rather than transgress God's commandments. No doubt these two passages—particularly the second, with its emphasis on exaltation after humiliation and the attention paid to the effects of the servant's sufferings for others—could have served very well the purpose of those who wanted to determine the meaning of Jesus' death.

However, notwithstanding J. Jeremias's careful listing of all the possible references and allusions to the texts, words, phrases, and ideas found in Isa. 52:13–53:12 in the writings of the New Testament, the evidence for the use of this passage in early Christianity is slight. In Acts 8:32–33 the Ethiopian eunuch reads Isa. 53:7–8 and Philip, in vv. 34–36, explains to him that the prophet is referring to Jesus. The hymn in 1 Peter 2:21–25, inserted in an exhortatory context, incorporates phrases from the Deutero-Isaianic passage. But both these texts are late. The use of the designation "the servant of the Lord" in Matt. 12:18–21 (quoting Isa. 42:1–4 in a special form) does not necessarily evoke the image of the *suffering* servant of Isa. 53, and the same is true of this expression in Acts 3:13, 26.

Next, there are stray quotations, of Isa. 52:15 in Rom. 15:21; of 53:1 in Rom. 10:16; and of 53:4 in Matt. 8:17. In no instance is there any reference to vicarious suffering. The last quotation, "he took our infirmities and bore our diseases," refers to Jesus' healings and his exorcisms. Only in the Lukan Passion narrative do we find a reference to Isa. 53:12, "he was numbered with the transgressors" (22:37). In the earlier material we find that the use of the term "many" in Mark 10:45; 14:24 is often thought to have been influenced by Isa. 53:11–12, but it is very difficult to prove this conclusively. On the other hand, it is likely that the wording of Rom. 4:25 was influenced by Isa. 53:12 LXX, but here we have a particular, probably Pauline variant of the more general surrender formula.[31]

All in all, we shall have to conclude that the influence of Isa. 52:13–53:12 on the earliest Christian kerygma can hardly be demonstrated. A fortiori there is no proof that Jesus himself was profoundly or uniquely influenced by this scriptural passage.

## Jesus as the Son of Man

For T. W. Manson, Jesus is the Son of man par excellence, the embodiment of the Israelite ideal as portrayed in Daniel 7. Although Manson did not enter into any detailed analysis of the use of the Fourth Servant Song in early Christianity in general, or in the recorded words of Jesus in particular, the notion of the suffering servant occupies a central place in his writings. He defines the Son of man in terms of the Servant of the Lord described in Deutero-Isaiah. Typical for Manson is the emphasis on the corporate aspects of both the Son of man and the Servant of the Lord. Not only is the Son of man in Daniel's vision the symbolic representative of "the people of the Saints of the Most High" (Dan. 7:18, 22, 25, 27); also in the Parables of Enoch (1 En. 37–71) there is what Manson called an oscillation between the individual and the corporate, so that in chapters 70–71 the exalted Enoch is identified with the Son of man.[32] A similar oscillation is found in the authentic instances of the term in the synoptic gospels. Influenced by Daniel 7, Jesus could use the term for a community comparable to "the people of the Saints of the Most High"; at the same time "this corporate entity is embodied par excellence in Jesus himself, in such a way that his followers, who together with him constitute the Son of Man, may be thought of as extensions of his personality, or as St. Paul puts it later on, limbs of his body."[33] Daniel 7 emphasizes that it is the destiny of the Son of man to receive the Kingdom (vv. 14, 18, 22, 27). In this way the Israelite ideal is linked to the Davidic hope; Jesus deliberately chose to interpret the term Son of man in terms of the Servant of the Lord and thereby redefined the idea of the Messiah.[34]

Few would deny that the fate of Jesus' disciples is pictured as closely connected with that of their master and that corporate notions are very important in early Christian thought; I have pointed this out repeatedly in discussing the three models of interpretation. Yet Manson's interpretation of Son of man as a corporate entity also in the synoptic usage of the term has found very little support. Moreover, in view of the scarcity of explicit references to Isa. 52:13–53:12 or any of the other passages about the Servant of the Lord, it is highly questionable to interpret Son of man in terms of Servant of the Lord.

C. K. Barrett, criticizing Manson on this point,[35] has therefore tried to interpret the various Son of man sayings in the synoptic gospels, speaking about suffering as well as glory, with the help of the picture given in Daniel 7, studied in the context of the entire Book of Daniel. He claims that "independent of these gospel sayings . . . the Son of man figure is in himself bound up with the idea of suffering (and suffering embraces both an earthly life and an earthly death), and equally with the idea of heavenly glory." This approach is also found in M. D. Hooker's *The Son of Man in Mark*,[36] published in the same year as Barrett's Shaffer Lectures, as well as in G. N. Stanton's *Jesus of Nazareth in New Testament Preaching* (as has already been noted in the first chapter). According to M. D. Hooker, in Daniel, 1 Enoch, and basically also in Mark, "the Son of man is not simply one who appears at the end of time to act as judge: rather it is because he is Son of man now—i.e. elect, obedient, faithful and therefore suffering—that he will be vindicated as Son of man in the future: the eschatological role of the Son of man is based upon his obedient response to God now."[37]

Much has been written about the Son of man figure in early Jewish literature and the gospels, and there is great diversity of opinion on the development of the tradition, on the authenticity of the sayings, and on the question of whether Jesus used the term, and if so, in what sense. Let me, without further discussion of others, try to sum up what seems to me to be assured fact or at least reasonable deduction.[38]

The designation Son of man is found only in the four gospels and once in Acts; with the exception of John 12:34 and Acts 7:56 it is always given by Jesus himself. The very unusual Greek expression represents Semitic idiom; invariably the definite article is used: "*the* Son of man."[39] The expression is not found in Paul, let alone in the traditional material incorporated in his letters, nor in later writings of the New Testament. Only in Rev. 1:13 and 14:14 does "one like a son of man" occur, clearly influenced by Dan. 7:13. At a later stage, in discussion with a non-Jewish audience, Son of man clearly was no longer a suitable designation to explain Jesus' dignity and his relationship to God and man.

In the gospels only Jesus uses this expression, and it is, I think, always in reference to himself—though this has been disputed. In Mark it is used to indicate Jesus' authority on earth. The Son of man has authority to forgive sins (2:10), and he is Lord even of the sabbath (2:28). The designation is used when Jesus predicts his death and resurrection (8:31; 9:9–12; 9:31; 10:33), or his death alone (14:21, 41). He uses it when he speaks about his future coming in glory (8:38; 13:26; 14:62); in the last two texts there is a clear allusion to the coming of "one like a son of man" in Dan. 7:13–14; and in 8:38–9:1 and 14:62 there is a link with the coming of the future Kingdom of God. The use of this designation in Q is less explicit. There is no reference to suffering and death and no direct connection with Dan. 7:13. It is stated, however, that the Son of man is sent by God with authority and expects people to give careful attention to his message. Some people give up everything and follow him; the people of "this generation" reject him (see Luke 7:34, par. Matt. 11:19; Luke 9:58, par. Matt. 8:20; Luke 11:30, Matt. 12:40 [slightly different]). Those who obey him will be vindicated: "And I tell you, every one who acknowledges me before men, the Son of man also will acknowledge before the angels of God; but he who denies me before men will be denied before the angels of God" (Luke 12:8–9, par. Matt. 10:32–33). The designation "Son of man" is here clearly connected with the future judgment (though the Son of man is not expected to act as judge himself). The future Son of man is also found in Luke 12:40

(par. Matt. 24:44); 17:22, 24, 26, 30 (par. Matt. 24:27, 37, 39). These texts speak about the sudden arrival of the Son of man; the disciples should be watchful and prepared, unlike the people of this generation, who continue their all-too-human pursuits.

We cannot vouch for the authenticity of each individual saying about the Son of man, even in Mark and Q. But the fact that this unusual Greek expression is used—and is used exclusively in words of Jesus, whereas early Christians did not employ it in their own preaching (except when words of Jesus were concerned)[40]—makes it likely that "Son of man" belongs to the oldest layers of tradition, if not to Jesus' own vocabulary.

If Jesus did use this term himself, what did he mean by it? Much has been written about the possible meanings of the Aramaic expression *bar (e)nash(a)* in Jesus' time. Was it used as a circumlocution for "I" or in general statements in which the speaker could, at times, include himself, or did it denote a class of persons with whom the speaker identified himself ("a man like myself")?[41] A number of Greek sayings are often considered to be the result of misunderstanding and consequent mistranslation. At the later stages of transmissions of the sayings represented by Mark and Q, however, the term Son of man is in any case used as an exclusive self-reference.

At the same time it does not unequivocally disclose the identity of the speaker. Nowhere in the gospels do those who respond to Jesus positively declare, "You are the Son of man!"—though they do confess him as the Messiah (so Peter, for instance, in Mark 8:29)—and nowhere do his opponents take him up on this self-designation—though in Mark 14:61 the high priest asks Jesus explicitly, "Are you the Christ, the Son of the Blessed?"[42]

Mark and Q clearly do not regard Son of man as a title readily understood (and then misunderstood when used in connection with Jesus) by all. This agrees with the fact that (contrary to what is often thought) we do not find a proper titular use of the expression anywhere in contemporary Judaism. The central figure in the Parables of Enoch (1 En. 37–71) is called Son of man only where the expression "one like a Son of man" from Dan. 7:13–14 is referred to, or where further qualifications are added. The Parables of Enoch are difficult to date; they may be as late as the end of the first century C.E.,[43] roughly around the time when another apocalypse, 4 Ezra, was written. Here the picture of the central figure in chapter 13 is clearly influenced by Daniel 7, but nowhere is "Son of man" used as a title.

This state of affairs makes it likely that Jesus did in fact speak of himself as "the Son of man," a designation not directly understood by outsiders, but for him and for insiders referring to "the one like a Son of man" in Daniel 7, understood in the way suggested by Barrett, Hooker, and Stanton. In any case the designation implied obscurity, homelessness and rejection, humility, service, suffering, and ultimately death; also authority (disputed, however, until the disclosure of Jesus' true identity) and, of course, final vindication at the full realization of God's sovereign rule on earth.[44] In view of our consideration of Jesus as servant, we may say with some confidence that the term Son of man applied by Jesus to himself had the connotation of suffering, death, and vindication of the obedient servant of God par excellence, who appeared at a crucial moment in the history of Israel and the world. To what extent further details in the Son of man–sayings in Mark and Q (and elsewhere) reflect Jesus' own views escapes our knowledge.

The three models of interpretation of Jesus' death found in the earliest layers of traditional material can all provide some insight into Jesus' own understanding of his life and death, as well as into the Christology of his earliest followers. Jesus may have interpreted rejection and possible death as that of God's final envoy to Israel. It is also probable that he saw himself as an obedient suffering servant who would be vindicated by God; my analysis of the use of the term Son of man in Mark and Q has given support to this thesis. It is impossible to say with certainty whether Jesus regarded his death as a dying for others, along the lines of martyrdom found in 2 and 4 Maccabees, but it is certainly possible that he did so.

In all instances the early Christian models of interpretation take for granted that Jesus' death was that of one who was related to God in a unique way and that it brought about a definitive and lasting change in the relationship between God and those faithful to him. Jesus' death, followed by his vindication and exaltation, had inaugurated a new era: this conviction connected the Christology that developed after Easter with the eschatology proclaimed before Easter.

# IV

# *Jesus*
# *as Inaugurator*
# *of the Kingdom*
# *of God*

Jesus' death, followed by his resurrection, was thought by his followers to mark the beginning of a new era in the relationship between God and humanity. The death of Jesus as God's final messenger to Israel had brought about a definitive change in God's relationship to that people; his final judgment on its leaders, who had rejected Jesus (and his messengers), had become inevitable. As God's suffering righteous servant and Son of God par excellence, Jesus had been vindicated by God when he was raised from the dead; he would come in the glory of his Father to reveal his kingdom in power. When Jesus died for all who placed their trust in him, he effected reconciliation and redemption forever.

This aspect of definitive, eschatological change is not inherent in the early Christian models of interpretation. It is a reasonable supposition that after his death Jesus' followers were firmly convinced that a new era had dawned in his victory over death *because they already believed in the inauguration of God's sovereign rule by Jesus during his mission on earth.* This mission might have seemed to fail, but now it had become clear that it was continuing. Even his death had become an instrument in drawing people to God and making them partners in God's new covenant.

If Jesus' disciples believed that he was the herald and inaugurator of God's Kingdom, the growing opposition to his message must have led them to envisage the likelihood of suffering and death and to contemplate the possibility of divine intervention and vindication. Many have thought that Jesus himself was firmly convinced of his mission as herald and inaugurator of God's Kingdom (see chapter 1). In that case he, too, must have considered the likelihood of persecution and death, and believed that it would be meaningful in God's eyes. He must have been convinced that his preaching and actions would not be in vain but would be vindicated by God. However difficult it is to speak with certainty in these matters, there must also have been some measure of continuity between the beliefs concerning Jesus (both before and after Easter) and Jesus' own views on his mission.

My focus in this chapter will be on this continuity between Jesus and his followers. My first question will be to what extent the belief in Jesus' inauguration of God's rule on earth influenced the conviction that God had made a new start by raising Jesus from the dead. Together with this I shall examine whether the notion of the "messianic woes" influenced the views of Jesus' followers on his and on their own sufferings, and whether this sheds any light upon Jesus' own announcements of death and resurrection. Next I shall ask if Jesus' own announcement of God's Kingdom, with its dynamic tension between present and future, implied a claim concerning his own person. If so, the question arises: were certain designations used for him or even by him, even before the events around and after his death led to a more developed Christology?

## RESURRECTION AND SUFFERING AS COLLECTIVE EVENTS

It has often been argued that the expression "to raise from the dead" is to be understood primarily against the backdrop of the apocalyptic and pharisaic conceptions of the resuscitation of the dead at the end of time. This point of view has been put forward eloquently and clearly by Helmut Merklein in an article on the raising of Jesus and the beginnings of Christology.[1] He starts with one of the oldest resurrection formulas, "God raised him [Jesus] from the dead" (Rom. 10:9; 1 Cor. 6:14; 15:15; 1 Thess. 1:10), and the clause "who raised him [Jesus] from the dead" (Rom. 4:24; 8:11; 2 Cor. 4:14; Gal. 1:1, cf. Col. 2:12; Eph. 1:20) used as a predicate to specify God's acts. The emphasis is on God, who by raising Jesus shows that he is able to make a new beginning and create new life. In Romans 4 Paul first mentions as an example Abraham's belief in the God "who gives life to the dead and calls into existence the things that do not exist" (v. 17; cf. Benediction 2 of the Eighteen Benedictions) and then ends the chapter with a reference to "us who believe in him that raised from the dead Jesus our Lord, who was put to death for our trespasses and raised for our justification" (vv. 24–25).[2]

The God who raised Jesus is the God who gives life to the dead, as will become evident in the final resurrection. The early Christians were well aware of the fact that only Jesus had been raised so far, but his resurrection formed the basis of their expectation that all believers would be raised. "God raised the Lord and will also raise us up by his power," says Paul in 1 Cor. 6:14 (cf. 2 Cor. 4:14; Rom. 8:11; 1 Thess. 4:13–18). This is brought out most clearly in the long chapter 1 Corinthians 15, where (among other things) he declares that "in fact Christ has been raised from the dead, the first fruits of those who have fallen asleep" (v. 20, see also vv. 22–23; cf. Rom. 8:29; Col. 1:18; Acts 26:23; Rev. 1:5).

The apostle uses corporate notions that stress the close connection between Jesus and those who belong to him in order to explain how their resurrection is based on his. As I have already argued, these corporate notions may be early, but Paul's conclusions about the significance of Jesus' resurrection are very likely his own. Merklein rightly regards what he calls the *Begründungszusammenhang* between the statement that Jesus was raised from the dead and the general resurrection as secondary rather than original. He posits, therefore, that Jesus' resurrection was understood not only against the background of the resurrection at the end of time but also in terms of the exaltation of God's suffering righteous servants.[3] This interpretation made it easier to apply the notion of eschatological resurrection to the raising of the one man Jesus, since history clearly had not yet reached its end.

If it is true that the followers of Jesus needed more than one concept to express their convictions concerning what God had done for their teacher after his death, and if the terms used to denote "raising up/resurrection" in themselves could evoke different associations,[4] there is room for another approach than that put forth by Merklein. If an interpretation in terms of a general resurrection was facilitated by the notion of the exaltation of a righteous one, it is worth asking whether the emphasis lay on the first or on the second notion. Since a question like this can probably never be answered satisfactorily, it seems more likely that from the very beginning an "opalescent"[5] notion of resurrection led to a many-faceted approach to Jesus' death and resurrection. One thing, however, stands out clearly, in my opinion. The post-Easter belief that God's vindication of Jesus had ushered in a new era (a new era that was already manifesting itself in the lives of his followers and that would culminate in their resurrection at the end of time) would never have received such prominence if the dynamic presence of the Kingdom of God had not been recognized in Jesus even before Easter, and if this had not led to the expectation that its complete realization was at hand.

Dahl's view, outlined in chapter 1, is that the events of Easter and Pentecost were explained and experienced as the preliminary fulfillment of Jesus' eschatological promise; otherwise one would have had to admit that this promise, at the heart of his message, remained unfulfilled. Stanton and Hahn have a similar perspective. A few remarks by Petr Pokorný are also in order here. He reminds us that the resurrection of one particular man, Jesus, was the keystone of early Christian belief: "We may have stressed that the oldest statements of faith, on the one hand, and the later written and formulated reports of the appearances, on the other, testify to the event that inaugurates the new reality, but we have to add straight away that the new reality is bound up with Jesus of Nazareth."[6] The risen one had to be identified with the earthly Jesus, Pokorný argues. "So far as the content is concerned, the preaching of Jesus is, despite all the differences, so intimately bound up with the Easter message that it became the way in which the later personal identification of the resurrected one with the earthly Jesus was shown to be the inwardly logical consequence of the experience of faith."[7]

Dale C. Allison has recently raised a related matter with some force in *The End of the Ages Has Come: An Early Interpretation of the Passion and Resurrection of Jesus.*[8] "Jesus' resurrection," he argues, "was interpreted not as an isolated event but as part of the general resurrection of the dead, and his death was understood as if it were a death in the great tribulation of the latter days" (p. 100). The first half of this assertion is clearly more problematic than its simple formulation suggests, but what about the second half? Does it point to a model of interpretation of Jesus' death to which we have as yet paid too little attention?

The problems Allison encounters in substantiating his second contention are manifold. The announcement of a period of great tribulation marking the transition between the present time and the age to come is widespread in Judaism, but it is by no means found everywhere. It does not always occupy an important place, and there is a great diversity in detail, as Allison himself points out.[9] There is also no fixed terminology: the term "the woes of the Messiah," often mentioned in connection with Mark 13:8 and Col. 1:24, is found only in later, rabbinic sources.[10] It is by no means self-evident that Jesus and his earliest followers should have used this complex idea in interpreting either the conflict and death they expected or the distress they were currently experiencing.

There is also a great variety in early Christian use of eschatological language and in the attempts by individual authors to express the many facets of God's definitive action on behalf of humanity as manifested in Jesus' death and resurrection. The part of the book most relevant for our present purpose is Allison's discussion of the evidence of the Pauline letters.[11] He correctly points out that Paul, convinced that the appointed time has grown very short, speaks of "the present [*or* impending] distress" (1 Cor. 7:26). Christians, Paul says, are children of God and fellow-heirs with Christ, "provided we suffer with him in order that we may also be glorified with him" (Rom. 8:17), and the "sufferings [*pathēmata*] of this present time are not worth comparing with the glory that is to be revealed to us" (v. 18)—a statement explained in the subsequent verses (19–25). The suffering of Christians in general and of the apostle himself are portrayed as directly connected with those of Christ. Underlining the effect of incorporation in Christ, Paul declares as his goal "that I may know him and the power of his resurrection, and may share his sufferings, becoming like him in his death, that if possible I may attain the resurrection from the dead" (Phil. 3:10–11). The expression "the sufferings of Christ" is also used in a subtle passage about suffering and comfort in 2 Cor. 1:3–7; it occurs in 1 Pet. 4:13; 5:1 (cf. 1:11; 5:9) and is probably implied in Col. 1:24, which speaks of "my sufferings for your sake" and Christ's afflictions.

Similar expressions are found elsewhere in Paul's letters (2 Cor. 4:10; 13:4; Gal. 6:17). The exact meaning of these texts is difficult to establish because of the subtlety and complexity of Paul's thought, but Allison is right when he remarks that "apostolic suffering and the sufferings of Christ are so closely bound together that they are both included in the one expression, 'the sufferings of Christ' " (p. 66); the question, however, is to what extent this expression can be connected with the variegated conception of the messianic woes, particularly when Allison links this with the notion that the resurrection of Christ, "the first fruits of those who have fallen asleep" (1 Cor. 15:20), was part of the general resurrection.

Paul's approach is more complicated than Allison suggests—regarding the interpretation both of Christ's resurrection and of his death. If the early Christian community saw itself as living in the time of great eschatological tribulation and looked for the general resurrection, it also knew of God's Spirit and dynamic power at work in the community. Speaking about the effects of baptism in Rom 6:3–11, Paul says that Christians have been baptized into Christ's death and can walk in newness of life (v. 4). The "not yet" implied in the words "we shall certainly be united with him in a resurrection like his" (v. 5) is directly connected with the "already": "You must consider yourselves dead to sin and alive to God in Christ Jesus" (v. 11). In 1 and 2 Corinthians the apostle repeatedly stresses his weakness, most movingly so in 2 Cor. 12:1–10, where he refuses to boast of the revelations granted to him. For the sake of Christ he is content with weaknesses, insults, hardships, persecutions, and calamities. "I will all the more gladly boast of my weaknesses," he says, "that the power of Christ may rest upon me" (v. 9). As J. Christiaan Beker has argued, the presence of the new age in the old, grounded in the fact that for Paul and other early Christians Christ's resurrection was an event of the past that determined their present condition, entailed modification of the concept of the escalation of evil in the last times.[12] And if the notion of the messianic woes is not applicable to the sufferings of Christians without strictures, it can also not be applied without important modifications to Christ's suffering and death to which, in Paul's view, the sufferings of his followers were closely related.

In his discussion of the connection between Jesus' own expectations concerning his death and the prospect of a great tribulation, Allison takes up a number of synoptic texts, some of which have already been mentioned briefly in the third chapter of this book.[13] He emphasizes that Jesus expected distress and affliction and that he "surely must have assumed that God would vindicate his cause notwithstanding the coming time of trouble" (p. 137)—also that "the Synoptics do not permit one to sever the sufferings of Jesus from the sufferings of his disciples" (p. 117). But does that mean that he shared the views of many of his contemporaries concerning the great tribulation? Allison thinks so, although he does not agree with Schweitzer that Jesus, at the final stage of his ministry, expected to take up *in his own person* all the afflictions of the final tribulation in order to bring about the arrival of the Kingdom.[14]

The evidence, however, does not all point in the same direction. On the one hand, if Jesus used the term Son of man, and if he associated that term with Daniel 7, it is very likely that "he thought of his coming death and resurrection as defined by the eschatological sequence of tribulation and vindication" (p. 137).[15] He must also have expected his disciples to share in this process. On the other hand, the predictions of a passion and resurrection found in Mark 8:31, 9:31, and 10:33–34 speak about Jesus alone, whereas elsewhere in Mark we find predictions concerning the disciples that speak of their share in the joy and the glory of the Kingdom after they have suffered in imitation of their master (8:34–9:1; 10:28–31; 35–45). And in Mark 14:25 Jesus' death is connected not with his resurrection but with his participation in the Kingdom of God (cf. Matt. 19:28, par. Luke 22:29–30, which speaks about the disciples).

Do these texts presuppose a direct connection between resurrection and the arrival of the Kingdom, and did Jesus then expect that his followers would suffer and rise together with him, and at the same time? Allison thinks so: "resurrection was primarily a collective category and for Jesus himself, talk of resurrection would almost certainly have been talk about eschatological matters, about the vindication of all the saints—just as the prospect of suffering was, in Jesus' proclamation, a collective category and part of the latter days" (p. 139).

Resurrection was not exclusively a collective category, however, and Jesus, while stressing the close link between his followers and himself, may have separated in time his own death and resurrection from that of (at least most of) his followers. It is also not certain that for him resurrection and realization of the Kingdom coincided. To me it seems certain that vindication was the central notion. It could be expressed in terms of the antithesis between death and resurrection, but it could also be presented in terms of God's final triumph, the realization of God's Kingdom in power. Resurrection was, of course, a precondition for partaking in God's glory,[16] but it does not follow that the coming of the Kingdom in power had to take place at the time of Jesus' expected resurrection.[17] The available evidence does not allow us to speak with greater certainty; any reconstruction of the history of the transmission of Jesus' sayings on this matter is bound to be tentative.

One further remark is in order. It is not only Paul who thinks in terms of "not yet" and "already"; in Jesus' own announcements of the arrival of the Kingdom elements stressing its future aspect are found side by side with those emphasizing its presence. The future Kingdom is not so much proleptically present in the sufferings of the period immediately preceding the end as breaking into the present age in Jesus' words and mighty actions.

## JESUS' ANNOUNCEMENT OF THE KINGDOM OF GOD AND HIS OWN PERSON

The majority of modern critics agree that the announcement of the arrival of God's Kingdom constitutes the heart of the teaching of the synoptic gospels and, indeed, of Jesus himself. This has already become clear in the short survey of research into the historical figure of Jesus presented in the first chapter. There is also considerable agreement as to the essentials of Jesus' message concerning the Kingdom. The situation has been summed up admirably by N. A. Dahl, who points out that we cannot go back beyond Albert Schweitzer's conclusion that "the eschatological message and the eschatological expectation bind Jesus and primitive Christianity into a unity." At the same time it is important to correct Schweitzer's "throroughgoing eschatology" by reminding ourselves that in Jesus' "own mission, his word and his work, God's Kingdom was already breaking in."[18]

In contemporary Jewish expectations as well (apocalyptic and otherwise) the decisive change hoped for was already inherent in the present.

People regarded themselves as caught up in a course of events that, thanks to God's righteousness and faithfulness, would inevitably lead to a judgment upon the world and a new dispensation in which his servants would share. One had to be prepared to repent and to lead a life of strict obedience to God's laws in order to survive the impending crisis. One dared not delay in one's preparations; reading the signs of the times one could expect God's intervention any time in the near future—although it remained in God's power to determine the exact time.[19]

Jesus' message is characterized by the same urgency; the element of *Naherwartung* (the expectation of the speedy complete realization of God's sovereign rule on earth) is evident. The saying "But of that day or that hour no one knows, not even the angels in heaven, nor the Son, but only the Father" (Mark 13:32) does not postpone events to a distant future. It is followed by the admonition, "Take heed, watch; for you do not know when the time will come" (Mark 13:33). Many early Christians shared their Master's expectation of a short-term realization of the new dispensation; as is well known, Paul was one of them. In his first letter, 1 Thessalonians, he expects to be alive at the coming of the Lord (1 Thess. 4:13–18), and later in his letter to the Romans he writes: "For salvation is nearer to us now than when we first believed; the night is far gone, the day is at hand" (Rom. 13:11b–12). For Paul the message concerning the (impending) fulfillment of what has been announced is founded in what God has already done in Jesus Christ, "For since we believe that Jesus died and rose again, even so, through Jesus, God will bring with him those who have fallen asleep" (1 Thess. 4:14). The certainty concerning what has taken place determines and intensifies the hope for what is sure to happen soon.[20]

The same is true with Jesus. Notwithstanding his links with John the Baptist, God's final prophet announcing God's judgment and urging repentance, he is more than John and he has a different message. To borrow a few phrases from Helmut Merklein in another clear and straightforward article, "Jesus, Künder des Reiches Gottes,"[21] John showed Israel the possibility to escape from the impending doom, but Jesus announced a new divine initiative, a new reality, new salvation. He urged people to accept what God offers, here and now.

Yet our necessary emphasis on the present aspects of God's Kingdom in Jesus' teaching should not induce us to fail to appreciate the future aspects and the intrinsic connection between present and future in the announcements of the Kingdom. I have already described (in chapter 1) T. W. Manson's one-sided approach to the problem. C. H. Dodd, with whom he agreed in this matter, explained away the future elements of Jesus' message by taking them as a figure of speech. In *The Parables of the Kingdom* he writes, "It appears that while Jesus employed the traditional symbolism of apocalypse to indicate the 'other-worldly' or absolute character of the Kingdom of God, He used parables to enforce and illustrate the idea that the Kingdom of God had come upon men there and then" (p. 197).

Dodd's and Manson's stress on "realized eschatology" betrays uneasiness about the meaning and relevance of apocalyptic imagery. It is interesting to note that in this respect they resemble R. Bultmann, notwithstanding his very different approach to the study of the synoptic gospels (see chapter 2). Amos Wilder's criticism of Bultmann's approach also applies to Dodd and Manson. We cannot do justice to the expectations of Israel or to Jesus' message if we do not take very seriously that they all were convinced that God would effectively intervene in human history and would judge and transform his creation.[22]

In many passages, in Q as well as in Mark, "the dynamic presence of the Kingdom of God in the words and deeds of Jesus receives emphasis. What happens through him and around him cannot but lead to the full realization of God's sovereign rule on earth expected to take place in the near future on God's initiative. . . . In view of the unanimity of our sources in mentioning both aspects we have to assume that he spoke about the Kingdom as a dynamic entity, both present and yet to be fully realized, and—very important—that he acted on that conviction."[23] The many sayings about the Kingdom of God have received extensive treatment elsewhere;[24] for our present purpose it seems worthwhile to summarize some important points.

First, we should note Jesus' announcement of the fulfillment of time and the nearness of the Kingdom in Mark 1:15, Jesus' answer to the disciples of John the Baptist—"Go and tell John what you have seen and heard!" in Q (Luke 7:18–23, par. Matt. 11:2–6)—and the first beatitude, also in Q (Luke 6:20)—"Blessed are you poor, for yours *is* the kingdom of God" (emphasis added), combined with the following two promising to those who hunger that they *shall* be satisfied, and to those who weep that they *shall* laugh (Luke 6:21). The parables of growth (or contrast: Mark 4:2–8, 26–29, 30–32, and others) illustrate that, however small and insignificant the beginning may seem, the end will be glorious and plentiful.

Jesus' message was addressed especially to the poor, the under-privileged, and the outcasts; and this message was borne out in his solidarity with them. He shared meals with tax collectors and sinners and was reproached for being their friend (Mark 2:14–17 and par.; Luke 7:34, par. Matt. 11:19 [Q]). The future Kingdom of God is also portrayed as a meal in which many will participate (Luke 13:28–29, par. Matt. 8:11–12; Luke 22:28–30, cf. Matt. 19:28; the two versions of the parable of the great feast in Luke 14:15–24 and Matt. 22:1–14).

Next, there are Jesus' healings and exorcisms, evidence of God's power acting through Jesus in order to destroy the dominion of Satan (Mark 3:22–30). Q has handed down a word of Jesus linking the exorcising of demons with the arrival of God's Kingdom: "But if it is by the finger of God that I cast out demons, then the kingdom of God has come upon you" (Luke 11:20; the parallel Matt. 12:28 reads "by the Spirit of God").

Above all Jesus acts as a person with authority. He calls people and they leave everything to follow him (e.g., in Mark 1:16–20, 2:14). Mark relates that after his very first public appearance at Capernaum people wonder who he is. He teaches with authority, and not as the scribes. He commands even the evil spirits and they obey him (Mark 1:21–28). He forgives sins (Mark 2:10) and interprets the law in a radical, new way (Matt. 5:21–48, cf. Luke 6:27–36; Mark 7:1–23, par. Matt. 15:1–20), claiming to interpret the essence of God's commandments over and against the human traditions cherished by his opponents. However we may reconstruct the course of events connected with Jesus' final con-frontation with the authorities in Jerusalem, we may safely say that the central issue at stake was Jesus' claim to authority.[25] Either he spoke and acted blasphemously (Mark 2:7; 14:64) or he spoke with a special mandate from God ("from heaven," Mark 11:27–33). Either he cast out demons as servant of the prince of demons or he did so inspired and empowered by God's Holy Spirit (Mark 3:22–30). Either he is insane or he is one who does the will of God in a singular fashion (see the controversy with his relatives in Mark 3:21, 31–35).

Does Jesus' message concerning God's Kingdom, then, manifesting itself in his own words and deeds, imply a claim for himself? Does the fact that he presents the Kingdom as breaking forth now, in what he says and does, imply some form of Christology? At this point scholars proceed with utmost caution.

We have already encountered Bultmann's disinclination—beyond conceding that Jesus' call to decision implies a Christology—to investigate the continuity between the period before and after Easter in this highly important issue. It was the kerygma of the early Church that made the Proclaimer the Proclaimed. We have also seen that Bultmann's pupil Bornkamm called Jesus unique, in the sense that he claimed to come with God's definitive offer and appeal; yet Jesus did not claim any messianic titles for himself.[26] An important argument for the theory that Jesus did not use any *Hoheitstitel* is that they would have hedged in and, in fact, fixed Jesus' eschatological uniqueness, his claim to speak directly on behalf of God.

This opinion is also found outside the Bultmannian school. Well known is Eduard Schweizer's description of Jesus as the man who fits no formula ("der Mann, der alle Schemen sprengt"), leading to the conclusion that "in any case Jesus did not assume any current title with an exalted meaning" but that "Jesus keeps all the possibilities open; he refuses to use titles, which of necessity define and delimit, to make God's free action an object of human thought, placing it at the disposal of human mind."[27]

Yet there is also another aspect, well brought out by F. Hahn when he identified as the real secret of Jesus' mission his inner certainty that he stood in a very special relationship to God as his Father. Very interesting and in a way typical of much modern scholarship is H. Merklein's approach in "Jesus, Künder des Reiches Gottes." On the one hand, he says, it is clear that a decision regarding the message of the Kingdom leads to a decision regarding Jesus as proclaimer and representative of the Kingdom (p. 138; cf. p. 151). The Lord's Prayer (Luke 11:2–4, par. Matt. 6:9–13) shows that the prayer for the coming of the Kingdom is directly connected with the freedom to address God as Father. Jesus addresses God as Father and teaches his disciples to do the same. A new era has begun, and at the heart of it is this special, intimate relationship between Jesus and his Father (pp. 141–142, cf. pp. 151–152).[28]

On the other hand, Merklein is of the opinion that an explicit Christology making use of messianic titles did not originate before Easter, the event which made it clear that God had inaugurated a new era. He immediately adds, however, that this theory does not exclude but rather assumes that such an explicit Christology presupposes Jesus' word and work and the eschatological authoritative claim inherent to it.[29]

I think there is room for a different approach. The use of the terms *implicit* and *explicit* is helpful insofar as it expresses the element of continuity in the positive response to Jesus before and after Easter. But if we think of explicit Christology primarily as a Christology of titles, and titles as fixed concepts, as unequivocal terms defining Jesus' exact role in God's dealings with Israel and the world, then we are on the wrong track. Anyone studying the use of the so-called *Hoheitstitel* within and outside Judaism[30] is immediately struck by the diverse ways in which they are used in a variety of literary and historical contexts. Certain terms stand for different combinations of traditional concepts (often connected with certain texts from Scripture), adapted to the specific situations of the authors or of their readers. I do not see why Jesus should not have clarified his own ideas about his mission, meditating in silence, praying to his God, speaking to his disciples, with the help of terms used to denote special servants of God in Israel's expectations of the future—and why he should not have applied them to his particular situation in a highly individual way.

The term *Son of man*, as noted in the third chapter, was not used as a title in contemporary Judaism, nor did Jesus use it as a title for himself. Yet it is likely that what was related about "one like a Son of man" in Daniel 7 deeply influenced Jesus' thought about his mission and his destiny. His use of the term as a cryptic self-designation betrays a highly individual interpretation of an apocalyptic concept found in the scriptures.

A second remark is in order. The more stress is laid on the continuity between the eschatological expectations of Jesus' followers after Easter and those before, including the conviction that God's Kingdom was already dynamically present in the words and deeds of the earthly Jesus, the less likely it becomes that there was a clear discontinuity in the use of christological designations. Even during his lifetime, did Jesus' unique claim to authority not ask for explicit statements, both on the part of his followers and on his own part?

If an incipient explicit Christology is plausible in theory, are there any indications that it did in fact exist, and that Jesus himself admitted its legitimacy? In the two concluding sections I shall look at the use of the designations "Messiah/Christ" and "Son of God." Limiting myself to actual occurrences of the term Messiah/Christ, I again start with a comparison of the use of these designations in early formulas in Paul's letters, in Mark, and in Q, and attempt to "ask back" to Jesus himself.

## JESUS AS THE MESSIAH/CHRIST

The word *Messiah*—or, literally, "anointed one,"—is frequently used as a general designation for God's final envoy on earth at the inauguration of a new era,[31] but this seems to me to lead to confusion. The term *anointed one* occurs surprisingly seldom in Jewish sources around the beginning of the Common Era. If it is used at all to refer to someone playing a role in God's final intervention, it denotes an ideal Davidic king. Only at Qumran is the term connected a few times with the awaited high priest, and also once with a future prophet. It is not at all self-evident that the word *christos* should have become the central term to be used for Jesus in early Christianity.[32]

At what stage did it become so important? About half the occurrences of the term in the New Testament are found in the letters of Paul. Here, as N. A. Dahl has shown,[33] it is seldom used with a technical meaning. The designation Christ "receives its content not through a previously-fixed conception of messiahship but rather from the person and work of Jesus Christ." Already before Paul Jesus was called *christos,* particularly in connection with the formula "Christ died for us/you"—as noted in the preceding chapter. This appellation is also found in double formulas speaking about Jesus' death and resurrection (e.g., 1 Cor. 15:3–5, cf. 12–19). And, in general, *christos* stands for what is believed and proclaimed about Jesus, as "the Gospel" centering around his death and resurrection.

How then did this term come to be connected with Jesus' death and resurrection? Many have accepted Dahl's answer in yet another influential article, "The Crucified Messiah."[34] As Dahl aptly points out, "from the discovery of the empty tomb (if it is historical) and from the appearances of the Resurrected One it could be inferred that Jesus lives and is exalted to heaven. But from this it could not be inferred that he is the Messiah" (pp. 25–26). He continues: "If he was crucified as an alleged Messiah, then—but only then—does faith in his resurrection necessarily become faith in the resurrection of the Messiah. In this way the distinctiveness of the Christian idea of the Messiah, in contrast to the Jewish, was given from the outset" (p. 26).[35] Mark 15 tells us that Jesus was crucified as "King of the Jews"—that is, as one pretending to be the Messiah (see also Mark 14:61–62).

Dahl does not think that Jesus ever used this title for himself. But many of his more ardent followers certainly did. One should not speak of a "non-messianic history before the passion," but rather of "a movement of broken messianic hopes" (p. 32). It is not at all strange that the messianic hopes of Jesus' followers and his sovereign attitude to the Law and Jewish customs, coupled with severe criticism of the Jewish establishment, should have led the authorities to accuse him of royal-messianic claims. And Jesus "could not deny the charge that he was the Messiah without thereby putting in question the final eschatological validity of his whole message." By not denying it, he accepted the cross; "his willingness to suffer is implicit in Jesus' behavior and attitude throughout his preaching" (p. 33).

Dahl's caution is to be commended, but the weak point in his reconstruction is his theory that it was Jesus' opponents who made his messiahship the central question and forced Jesus to accept the charge "by his silence, if not in any other way," as Dahl puts it (p. 34). In his view, only their accusation and Jesus' reaction to it led to the adoption of the *christos*-title in early Christianity and to its obtaining a central position, directly connected with Jesus' death and resurrection.

I must confess that I find it difficult to accept that Jesus' opponents were able to make messiahship the decisive issue, while Jesus himself avoided this designation and discouraged his followers to use it in connection with him.[36] It is not so easy, however, to demonstrate that he did accept the title Messiah.

The term *christos* is not found in the sayings which can be attributed to Q, and it occurs only a few times in the Gospel of Mark. Among the crucial instances is Peter's confession "You are the Messiah/Christ" in 8:29, said to be elicited by Jesus himself. It constitutes a turning point in Mark's narrative, after the description of Jesus' activity in Galilee as a unique preacher, teacher, and exorcist at the turn of times. Jesus does not contradict this confession but commands his disciples to keep it secret (8:30). The first of the three predictions of Jesus' suffering, death, and resurrection follows immediately (8:31), with the designation "Son of man." For Mark the confession "Jesus is the Christ" presupposes the entire story of Jesus' death, resurrection, and finally the parousia (8:38). Jesus declares this openly in 14:61–62 in answer to the high priest's question, "Are you the Christ, the Son of the Blessed?" At that crucial moment, facing death, Jesus replies: "I am; and you will see the Son of man sitting at the right hand of power, and coming with the clouds of heaven." Earlier in the story Jesus praises the faith of the blind beggar Bartimaeus, whom he heals and accepts as his follower after Bartimaeus has addressed him as "Son of David" (10:46–52). At Jesus' entry into Jerusalem he is greeted as one "who comes in the name of the Lord" and associated with "the kingdom of our father David that is coming" (11:9–10). In 12:35–37 Jesus introduces the equation of the Messiah with the son of David as an opinion typically held by the scribes. Referring to Ps. 110:1, he points out that David calls him Lord. Although he does not explicitly refer to himself as the Messiah, readers of Mark will immediately note that Ps. 110:1 quoted here is also alluded to in Mark 14:61–62. For Mark Jesus is the Messiah, Son of David. He works on earth as a prophet, teacher, and exorcist; and in the future, after God has vindicated him, he will exercise the functions of the one like a Son of man of Daniel 7. Moreover, for Mark he is Son of God (8:38; 14:61–62, and other texts, to be discussed in the next section).[37]

The question remains, however, whether Mark's presentation of Jesus' reaction to the title *christos* reflects Jesus' own attitude or the early Christology also expressed in the early pre-Pauline formulas. It is important to remember that Isa. 11:1–5, "the Spirit of the LORD shall rest upon him, the spirit of wisdom and understanding, the spirit of counsel and might, the spirit of knowledge and the fear of the LORD," has exercised a considerable influence on Jewish expectations concerning the coming royal Son of David. A very conspicuous example is Ps. Sol. 17, often (one-sidedly) referred to as a typical example of the earthly and nationalistic messianic expectation. In the last part of this psalm (vv. 30–45) the king is portrayed as "strong with holy spirit, wise in the counsel of understanding with strength and righteousness" (v. 37).[38]

In the Old Testament David is not only king but also psalmist, prophet, and exorcist. In 1 Sam. 16:1–13 we hear how, immediately after Samuel had anointed him, "the Spirit of the LORD came mightily upon David from that day forward" (v. 13). The Spirit of the Lord departs from Saul, and it is David who by singing hymns makes the evil Spirit that torments the king depart (1 Sam. 16:14–23). In the introduction to the last words of David (2 Sam. 23:1–7) he is called, among other things, "the anointed of the God of Jacob," and David is recorded as saying, "The Spirit of the LORD speaks by me" (vv. 1–2).

Josephus, Ant. 6.166–168 describes David's exorcisms; Ps. Philo LAB 59–60 mentions new Davidic psalms in this connection, as does the 11 Q Psalms Scroll. This last source also includes a list of "David's compositions" that not only mentions an enormous number of psalms and hymns but also specifies that David composed four "songs for making music for the stricken." All his compositions were spoken "through prophecy given to him from before the Most High" (11 QPs^a Dav. Comp. vv. 9–11). Also in Mark 12:36 and in Acts 1:16 and 4:25 David is said to have spoken through the Holy Spirit, and in Acts 2:30 he is called a prophet.

Mark's characterization of Jesus' activity on earth as prophet, teacher and exorcist as that of "the Christ, Son of David" is very much in line, then, with the picture of David found in parts of the Old Testament and in some Jewish sources, as well as with certain expectations concerning the future ideal Son of David. The evangelist separates prophecy and exorcism from the royal aspects of the Messiah's activity, however; they are specifically connected with the period *after* Jesus' earthly life, when he will exercise royal power in the context of the realization of God's sovereign rule on earth (8:38–9:1; 14:62).

If Jesus' messiahship became an issue at his trial before Pilate only because the designation Messiah had earlier been used in connection with Jesus, and probably by Jesus himself, it is quite possible that

Mark's interpretation is accurate. Jesus may have understood himself as a prophetic Son of David called to proclaim the Gospel and exorcise demons in order to inaugurate God's Kingdom, and destined to hold full royal power in the near future. If so, he could regard himself as the Lord's anointed like David, not only in the future, but already during his prophetic work in Galilee.[39] This is how his disciples saw him, as Mark's clearly stylized, prototypical story of Peter's confession seeks to make clear. Jesus' messiahship could be and indeed was misunderstood by some of his followers and many of his opponents alike, but there is no reason to deny that he probably did regard himself as the Lord's anointed in the sense indicated.

Definitive proof cannot be adduced. But this reconstruction allows for continuity, also in the use of the designation Messiah, before and after Easter. It is certainly one-sided, if not wrong altogether, to connect the title Messiah exclusively with the display of royal power and then to state that Jesus could be called Messiah only after his vindication by means of his resurrection.[40] The Easter experiences affirmed earlier belief in Jesus as Christ and expectations concerning his future and that of those connected with him. The paradox that the Messiah sent to Israel had been put to death on the cross made an explanation of the meaning of his death a matter of urgency, as we have seen. This Messiah was, indeed, a servant-Messiah in a very special sense.

## JESUS AS THE SON OF GOD

Finally, we must ask if Jesus called himself Son of God and if it is possible to say something more about the special relationship between Jesus and God, whom he is reported to have called his Father.[41]

In the earliest Christian traditions accessible to us the term *Son of God* is used in different contexts with different connotations. In Gal. 4:4–5 Paul employs an ancient pattern of thought when he writes, "But when the time had fully come, God sent forth his Son, born of woman, born under the law, to redeem those who were under the law, so that we might receive adoption as sons." The ancient kernel is here: "God sent his Son in order that . . ."—found in Rom. 8:3–4, John 3:16–17, and 1 John 4:9 as well. It is also reflected in the parable of the vineyard in Mark 12:1–9: "He had still one other, a beloved son; finally he sent him to them" (v. 6). The emphasis is on the unique relationship between God and the Son whom he sends at the turn of times in order to bring about a fundamental change in the lives of those who accept him. The nature of that change can be expressed in different terms; for Paul and John the pattern implies pre-existence, but this is not the case in Mark, where it is combined with the concept of Jesus as God's final envoy rejected by Israel.[42]

In a number of other texts we find Son of God together with Son of David or Messiah (see, as mentioned in the preceding section, Mark 12:35–37; 14:61–62; Rom. 1:3–4). Here Son of God is associated especially with the period after the exaltation/resurrection (cf. also in Mark 8:38; 1 Thess. 1:9–10). This is also the case in Acts 13:33–34, where Ps. 2:7 is applied to Jesus' resurrection.[43]

These occurrences of Son of God should be seen in the context of the use of the term to denote the Davidic king in Old Testament texts (2 Sam. 7:12–14; Ps. 2:7; Ps. 89:3–4, 26–27; 1 Chron. 17:13; 22:10; 28:6).[44] The special connection between sonship and resurrection may have been inspired by the prophecy attributed to Nathan in 2 Sam. 7:12–14: "I will raise up your offspring after you. . . . I will establish the throne of his kingdom for ever. . . . I will be his father, and he shall be my son."[45] But in view of the interpretation of the term Messiah outlined above, it seems doubtful that Jesus' sonship would have been regarded as beginning only with his exaltation, even where that is stressed. After Jesus' resurrection it became evident what he, as Son of David and Messiah, already was; it also became apparent that his reign was to last forever.

Paul and Mark successfully combined this tradition about the royal Son of God with the strand of thought which implies that Jesus was Son of God from the very moment his mission began. In the Passion story Mark, too, incorporates the conception of the exemplary righteous servant as son of God (see chapter 3) found in Wisd. Sol. 2:12–20; 5:1–7; see Mark 15:29–32 (and especially Matt. 27:39–44) and 15:39 (par. Matt. 27:54; Luke 23:47); he even takes one further important step by attributing the introduction of the term Son of God into the story of the Gospel to God himself. It is God who declares, "Thou art my beloved Son," when Jesus is baptized and receives the Spirit (1:10–11), and it is God who confirms this, saying, "This is my beloved Son;

listen to him," at the transfiguration (9:7). For Mark, Jesus' sonship is
rooted in a special relationship inaugurated by God himself.[46] Human
beings may not be aware of it (in fact, Jesus' three most intimate
disciples know this only because it is revealed to them at the transfiguration), but the demons recognize the Son of God who is mightier than
they themselves (3:11; 5:7; cf. 1:24).

In Mark, Jesus is also portrayed as addressing God as Abba, Father.
At Gethsemane he prays: "Abba, Father, all things are possible to thee;
remove this cup from me; yet not what I will, but what thou wilt"
(14:36). The Aramaic word *abba* was used in early Christian prayers, as
Paul shows in Gal. 4:4–7. God sent his Son, he says, in order that we
might receive adoption as sons. He continues: "And because you are
sons, God has sent the Spirit of his Son into our hearts, crying 'Abba!
Father!' " (v. 6; cf. Rom. 8:14–17). We may assume that this reflects an
ancient usage, rooted in the tradition that Jesus himself called God
"Father" and that he taught his disciples to pray in the same way.[47]

The centrality of the relationship to God as Father is clearly evident
in the Lord's Prayer, which belongs to the Q-material (Luke 11:4, par.
Matt. 6:9–13), and it also comes to expression in another important
Q-passage, Luke 10:21–22 (par. Matt. 11:25–27). This passage,
which opens with the words, "I thank thee, Father, Lord of heaven and
earth," stresses the unique relationship between the Father and the
Son, to whom all real knowledge of God is imparted in order that he
may reveal it to those he chooses. I cannot treat this frequently discussed passage in detail here. This much is clear, however: the relationship between Father and Son pictured here goes beyond that of the
truly righteous man who is called son of God in Wisd. Sol. 2:13, 16–18.
It is closer to that between (female) Wisdom and God in Wisd. Sol. 8:3–
4 (cf. 9:9):

> "She glorifies her noble birth by living with God,
> and the Lord of all loves her.
> For she is an initiate in the knowledge of God,
> and an associate in his works."

Jesus is more than a supremely wise and righteous man or the ideal
representative of Wisdom on earth. He addresses God as Father and
speaks and acts out of his very special union with God. Luke 10:21–22

may represent the very core of Jesus' relationship to God, which goes beyond the use of any special title.[48] Yet here, too, continuity exists between the early Christology expressed in the words "Jesus is the Son of God" and Jesus' own expression of his relationship to his Father.

Jesus not only announced the Kingdom of God; he inaugurated it. This placed him in a unique relationship to God, and he was aware of it when he addressed God as Father. It is probable that he regarded himself as the Messiah and Son of David inspired and empowered by the Spirit. We do not know whether he called himself Son of God, but he certainly spoke and acted as the Son on whom the Father had bestowed everything to be his servant at a supreme moment: the long-awaited turning point in human history.

# *Jesus*
# *at the*
# *Crossroads*
# *of Traditions*

Once early Christology is taken seriously as a response to *Jesus*, it must be asked why people responded to Jesus in the ways they did. What concepts, "models," and "myths" did they use, and why did they connect them with Jesus to express his function and position in God's dealings with humanity? In order to answer these questions a critical analysis of traditions, with reference to continual change *and* continuity, is necessary. Development in the various strands in the early response to Jesus must be examined carefully with a view to determining its earliest stages. In order to outline with some degree of probability Jesus' own views concerning his relationship to God and the nature of his mission, it is necessary to "ask back," starting from the earliest forms of response.

At the same time it is necessary to examine the concepts used by early Christians to express the meaning of Jesus' mission, including his death and resurrection, in the light of ideas and myths current among Jews living in a Hellenistic culture. Early Christian christological tradition is extremely variegated, and so is the Jewish—and in some (usually later) cases Hellenistic—material providing the background which helps us to understand early Christian terminology and ideas. Yet all the various strands of christological thinking, pursued backward, converge in Jesus. There must have been a reason why it was Jesus who was placed at the center, and why certain forms and concepts were chosen by his followers out of the many that were available in the religious and cultural context in which they lived. Jesus is found at the crossroads of traditions.

In approaching the situation, I have followed Nils A. Dahl's wise counsel to aim for a clear picture of what was typical and characteristic of Jesus by combining two methods: first, to make cross sections of the material found in different sources and genres of tradition and, second, to draw longitudinal lines leading from Judaism through Jesus to early Christianity. Dahl gave this advice as an alternative to radical criticism, which, by applying the criterion of dissimilarity, yields only a minimum of evidence. This minimum should, he felt, not be dogmatized but should be supplemented by the methods just mentioned to draw on the totality of the early Christian tradition concerning Jesus.

In chapters 3 and 4 I have tried to interpret the words of Jesus and stories about Jesus consistently as part of the early Christian tradition reflecting what Jesus said and did. Mark and Q, for the reasons given in chapter 1, were used on the same level as the early traditions in Paul. This amounts to an extension of the application of the criterion of multiple attestation and a practical neglect of the criterion of dissimilarity because of the tenuous nature of its results, both quantitatively and qualitatively. Even if applied along with the criterion of coherence, it leads to a dissecting of tradition into a number of isolated sayings patched together to form a reduced picture of Jesus. Traditio-historical studies in the manner of Dahl's cross-section method and his longitudinal approach do not yield historically assured details, but they draw lines pointing in certain directions, irrespective of the historicity of each point on the line. Although they take source criticism and form criticism seriously (just as they pay attention to the redactional elements in the gospels and letters), they concentrate on the various elements of the overall picture rather than on a critically assured minimum. Eugene Boring, discussing Dahl's cross-section method, concluded that "this line of argument may be helpful in sorting out earlier motifs from later ones, but it is less helpful when it comes to dealing with particular sayings." Speaking about the criterion of attestation in multiple forms (which Dahl couples to the criterion of attestation in multiple sources), he correctly remarks that "this criterion, of course, can only take us back to early elements in the tradition, not necessarily to Jesus himself."[1]

My discussion has concentrated on a relatively small number of central issues in the early Christian response to Jesus: the meaning of his death and resurrection, his teaching about the Kingdom of God, and the Christology implied by it. In each individual section the passages concerned could have been analyzed in greater detail and more texts—including those belonging to later documents or stages in the tradition—could have been adduced. The related scriptural and early Jewish material could have been treated in greater depth as well. It would also have been possible to include other, less central but still important aspects of early Christology.

Allowing that these chapters provide a sketch rather than a complete picture, we nevertheless can draw certain conclusions. A central point in the early Christian assessment of Jesus' death and resurrection is the strong conviction that these events marked a definitive and lasting change in God's relations with humankind, the beginning of a new era characterized by a dynamic tension between what had already begun and what would soon be realized more fully. I have argued that this conviction presupposes not only the certainty of Jesus' resurrection from the dead as proof of God's vindication of the one who had died ignominiously on the cross but also, and above all, continuity in the expectations concerning Jesus before and after Good Friday and Easter. Already during his earthly ministry Jesus' disciples must have been firmly convinced that he was not just a prophet but the final prophet, and that he not only announced the coming of God's Kingdom like a second John the Baptist but had inaugurated it through his own words and actions. Given the multiple attestation of Jesus' message concerning the Kingdom, we may assume that he himself did, in fact, claim to bring the Kingdom onto earth, modestly present now but soon to be realized in full power and glory.

If there was continuity in this central issue, we must assume that already during Jesus' ministry in Galilee and Jerusalem the question arose of how rejection and possible death could be reconciled with his mission to announce and inaugurate the Kingdom. Because it was imperative for early Christians to attempt to attach meaning to Jesus' death, it is not easy for us to sort out interpretation from history and go back beyond the formulas found in the Pauline tradition on this point. But a few things have become clear. First, it is evident that this question was an important one for Jesus' followers not only after but also before his death—if only because they served a master whose words and deeds aroused controversy, even rejection, and because they themselves faced the possibility of suffering and death. This was borne out particularly in my analysis of the view of Jesus as an envoy of God rejected by Israel. Going one step further, we may say that Jesus himself, faced with the opposition of leading and influential circles in Israel, must also have thought about the rejection he was destined to suffer in terms of the mission he was called to carry out. There is no reason why there should not have been continuity in attitude and interpretation between Jesus and his followers on this point and why Jesus himself should not have interpreted his fate as the rejection of God's final envoy. This, again, we find attested in multiple sources and multiple forms.

In the thoughts of Jesus and his followers, suffering and vindication must have been bound together right from the beginning, since death without subsequent vindication would have falsified Jesus' far-reaching message concerning God's Kingdom. The message of the resurrection is central to the early Christian kerygma, and it forms the climax of the story of Jesus told in the gospels. Jesus himself must have expected some sort of vindication from God, whether in terms of God's help for his righteous ones or of his raising up of martyrs to new life. For various reasons it is easier to present a case for Jesus' use of the first of these two models of interpretation than to prove that he regarded himself as a martyr. Unfortunately, in the latter case the evidence is rather one-sided; it is found only in pre-Pauline and other, liturgical formulas. Hence the criterion of multiple attestation fails us, and, clearly, the criterion of dissimilarity cannot be applied either.

This reconstruction of Jesus' views on his own death is open to differences of opinion, of course. In view of the absence of historically assured utterances of Jesus on this point which is so vital to the early Christian kerygma, historical research cannot attain certainty. Some readers will think that I have said too much; others may regard me as too cautious in my conclusions. My answer, for the moment, would be that I have tried to "ask back" as diligently as possible and to show that it pays to trace the continuity in the views of Jesus' followers before and after Easter, as well as the continuity in attitude and ideas between Jesus and his followers.

Too easily have scholars assumed the existence of an "unbridgeable gap" between the period before and after Easter, between Jesus' message concerning God and humankind on the one hand and the church's kerygma on the other. Many have also assumed a similar gap between the christological titles used by early Christians to refer to Jesus and Jesus' own claims to authority. In chapter 4 I have argued that here, too, far more continuity must have existed than is commonly assumed. It is generally agreed that Jesus' announcement of the Kingdom implied a Christology; yet the majority of New Testament scholars have regarded the use of christological titles by later Christians as an effort to define (in various ways) what in the end could not be defined, as a hedging-in of what transcended all boundaries of human thinking or imagination. Many scholars have felt that Jesus' uniqueness, in his message to humanity and in his relationship to God, was safeguarded by his avoidance of any particular designations.

I have also argued that "messianic" designations cannot be regarded as fixed (and therefore "fixing") concepts. They are fluid and adaptable within certain limits. Certain scriptural or other traditional ideas could be linked to a specific situation or a specific person. If there is reason to think that Jesus referred to himself as "the Son of man," then he may have been hinting at certain ideas about suffering and vindication that he knew from Daniel 7, and he may have applied them to his own person as well as to his followers. Given the variety in the use of the designation "the anointed one" and the many different features in the traditional image of David, the possibility cannot be excluded that Jesus, while avoiding popular political messianic ideas, did claim in his own way to be the Messiah, the Son of David. The variegated use of the designation "Son of God" in the gospels and in the Pauline tradition very likely reflects a distinct "Son-consciousness" on the part of Jesus—who encouraged and authorized his disciples to address God as "Our Father." It is not within a historian's competence to describe or define the exact nature of the Son-Father relationship between Jesus and God. But by pointing to parallels in the history of tradition and connecting them with different statements of early Christians concerning Jesus as Son of God, one may ascertain what calling Jesus "Son of God" must have conveyed and try to find indications as to Jesus' own, very personal use of the expression. Jesus may have expressed his own ideas about his personal relationship with God and his particular mission in terms traditionally used for special servants of God. He may have claimed this language in his own way—a way explained in his teaching and demonstrated in his actions, including his suffering and his self-sacrifice.

The approach I have taken in chapters 3 and 4 has its limitations. Even an intensified and broader investigation along the lines indicated there will never lead to a complete picture of Jesus' views of his calling and destiny. Our sources being what they are, we shall need multiple approaches, including one which takes into account that the Christians after Easter needed to find answers to many problems that had already existed beforehand. Once suffering and death became a real possibility, they had to be explained in terms of Jesus' message and mission—by Jesus' disciples and by Jesus himself.

Clearly we cannot assume that the interpretations of Jesus' death and resurrection found in various very early formulas occurring in Paul's letters, and expressed in the story of Jesus' crucifixion and resurrection as told in the gospels, are identical with Jesus' own interpretation(s). But it is not too rash to assume some continuity precisely with regard to this very central issue. Jesus inspired the early Christian kerygma centering around his death and resurrection not only by what he did and how he died but also by what he said about what was about to happen. The Proclaimer became the Proclaimed because of the very nature of his own proclamation. Jesus was the one with whom it all began.

# *Abbreviations*

Scriptural references are to the Revised Standard Version (RSV) unless otherwise noted.

## ANCIENT WORKS

### Old Testament

| | |
|---|---|
| Sam. | Samuel |
| Chron. | Chronicles |
| Ps. | Psalms |
| Isa. | Isaiah |
| Dan. | Daniel |

### New Testament

| | |
|---|---|
| Matt. | Matthew |
| Rom. | Romans |
| Cor. | Corinthians |
| Gal. | Galatians |
| Eph. | Ephesians |
| Phil. | Philippians |
| Col. | Colossians |
| Thess. | Thessalonians |
| Tim. | Timothy |

| | |
|---|---|
| Tit. | Titus |
| Heb. | Hebrews |
| Pet. | Peter |
| Rev. | Revelation |

### *Apocrypha and Pseudepigrapha*

| | |
|---|---|
| Wisd. Sol. | Wisdom of Solomon |
| Macc. | Maccabees |
| En. | Enoch |
| Ps. Sol. | Psalm of Solomon |
| Syr. Bar. | Syriac Apocalypse of Baruch |
| As. Mos. | Assumption of Moses |
| Ps. Philo LAB | Pseudo-Philo, Biblical Antiquities |

### *Dead Sea Scrolls*

| | |
|---|---|
| 4 QFlor | Florilegium from Qumran Cave 4 |
| 4 QpsDanA<sup>a</sup> | Pseudo-Danielic Text from Qumran Cave 4 (= 4Q246) |
| 11 QPs<sup>a</sup> Dav. Comp. | List of David's Compositions found in a Psalms Scroll from Qumran Cave 11 |

### *Josephus*

| | |
|---|---|
| Ant. | Antiquities of the Jews |

### MODERN WORKS

| | |
|---|---|
| BBB | Bonner biblische Beiträge |
| *BJRL* | *Bulletin of the John Rylands Library of Manchester* |
| CBNT | Coniectanea Biblica, New Testament |
| *ET* | *Expository Times* |
| FRLANT | Forschungen zur Religion und Literatur des Alten und Neuen Testaments |
| HDR | Harvard Dissertations in Religion |
| HTKNT | Herders theologischer Kommentar zum Neuen Testament |
| *HTR* | *Harvard Theological Review* |
| HTS | Harvard Theological Studies |

| *JTS* | *Journal of Theological Studies* |
| *NovT* | *Novum Testamentum* |
| *NTS* | *New Testament Studies* |
| OBO | Orbis biblicus et orientalis |
| QD | Quaestiones Disputatae |
| SBLMonS | Society of Biblical Literature Monograph Series |
| SBS | Stuttgarter Bibelstudien |
| SBT | Studies in Biblical Theology |
| SNT | Studien zum Neuen Testament |
| SNTSMS | Society for New Testament Studies Monograph Series |
| SPB | Studia Post Biblica |
| SPCK | Society for the Promotion of Christian Knowledge |
| SUNT | Studien zur Umwelt des Neuen Testaments |
| *TDNT* | *Theological Dictionary to the New Testament* |
| *TWNT* | *Theologisches Wörterbuch zum Neuen Testament* |
| WMANT | Wissenschaftliche Monographien zum Alten und Neuen Testament |
| WUNT | Wissenschaftliche Untersuchungen zum Neuen Testament |
| *ZNW* | *Zeitschrift für die neutestamentliche Wissenschaft* |
| *ZTK* | *Zeitschrift für Theologie und Kirche* |

### Miscellaneous Abbreviations

| B.C.E. | Before the Common Era |
| C.E. | Common Era |
| NEB | New English Bible |
| RSV | Revised Standard Version |

# *Notes*

1. Philadelphia: Westminster Press, 1988. The title and the concept of that book are the outcome of a long discussion (mainly by correspondence) with Wayne A. Meeks. For a number of earlier studies on Christology and on Messiah conceptions in early Judaism, see my "Earliest Christian Use of *Christos:* Some Suggestions," *NTS* 32 (1986), 321–343, esp. n. 35. (The essay "Two Messiahs in the Testaments of the Twelve Patriarchs," mentioned there, appeared in J. W. van Henten et al. (eds.), *Tradition and Reinterpretation in Jewish and Early Christian Literature: Essays in Honour of Jürgen C. H. Lebram* (SPB 36; Leiden: E. J. Brill, 1986), 150–162.

2. On this see *Christology in Context,* 20–21, 203–205.

3. See, for instance, chapter 3, "The Inquiry After the Man Jesus of Nazareth," in my *Jesus: Inspiring and Disturbing Presence,* trans. John E. Steely (Nashville and New York: Abingdon Press, 1974), 38–55, and *Christology in Context,* 21–26.

4. See *Christology in Context,* 84–88.

5. Not very much help is to be expected from the noncanonical material, of which there is considerably more since the discovery of the Nag-Hammadi Library—see, e.g., the various contributions in Charles W. Hedrick (ed.), *The Historical Jesus and the Rejected Gospels,* Semeia 44 (Atlanta: Scholars Press, 1988). In his introduction Hedrick argues that "standard critical studies clearly demonstrate a bias for that selected Jesus tradition out of which the Synoptic evangelists themselves constructed their own portraits of Jesus" (3). Four new sources should now be used: Papyrus Egerton 2

85

(1935), the *Gospel of Thomas*, the *Apocryphon of James*, and the *Dialogue of the Savior* (all from Nag-Hammadi). Less cautious than other contributors to the volume, Hedrick states: "Each of these texts presents a tradition that, to judge from recent research, derives not from the Synoptic Gospels, but rather from early Christian tradition, i.e., from the same sources that the Synoptic Gospels themselves derived their material" (5). This, of course, remains a hotly debated issue. Nonsynoptic origin will have to be demonstrated in the case of each individual saying, parable, or other item in this noncanonical material. We shall have to take this type of material seriously, but it is still too early to conclude that the apocalyptic element in the teaching of Jesus has to be reduced or discarded in favor of the Wisdom aspects, as Hedrick suggests.

6. This is evident in his article "The Life of Jesus: Some Tendencies in Present-Day Research," in W. D. Davies and D. Daube (eds.), *The Background of the New Testament and Its Eschatology: Studies in Honour of C. H. Dodd* (Cambridge: Cambridge University Press, 1954), 211–221. Between 1939 and 1953 Manson wrote no fewer than seven articles, brought together in Part One, "Materials for a Life of Jesus," of his *Studies in the Gospels and Epistles*, ed. M. Black (Manchester: Manchester University Press, 1962), 3–145. See also "Is It Possible to Write a Life of Christ?," *ET* 53 (1941–1942), 248–251.

7. On this see *The Servant-Messiah*, 52–53, and also "The Life of Jesus," 215–216, where Manson refers to C. H. Dodd's influential book *The Apostolic Preaching and Its Developments* (London: Hodder and Stoughton, 1936).

8. *Theology of the New Testament* (New York: Scribner's, 1951 and 1955), translation of *Theologie des Neuen Testaments* (Tübingen: J. C. B. Mohr, 1948–1953).

9. See Manson's review of the first two installments of the original German edition in *JTS* 50 (1949), 202–206, and New Series 3 (1952): 246–249.

10. See John Reumann, *Jesus in the Church's Gospels: Modern Scholarship and the Earliest Sources* (Philadelphia: Fortress Press and London: SPCK, 1968), and G. N. Stanton, *Jesus of Nazareth in New Testament Preaching* (SNTSMS 27; Cambridge: Cambridge University Press, 1974).

11. According to Manson (81), the cleansing of the Temple took place at the Feast of Tabernacles, Jesus' crucifixion at the Feast of Passover.

12. A. Schweitzer, *The Quest of the Historical Jesus* (New York: Macmillan, 1948), translation of *Geschichte der Leben-Jesu-Forschung*, 2d ed. (Tübingen: J. C. B. Mohr, 1913). See esp. chapter 21, which is devoted to "the solution of thoroughgoing eschatology." He earlier defended this thesis in *Das*

*Abendmahl im Zusammenhang mit dem Leben Jesu und der Geschichte des Urchristentums. II. Das Messianitäts- und Leidensgeheimnis* (Tübingen and Leipzig, J. C. B. Mohr, 1901), esp. chapter 9, "Das Geheimnis des Leidensgedankens" (pp. 81–98).

13. This is a key phrase in Dodd's *The Parables of the Kingdom* (London: Nisbet, 1935), based on the Shaffer Lectures for 1935. It indicates the conviction that Israel's expectations had become a reality in Jesus' ministry. Manson is also attracted by the term *sich realisierende Eschatologie* (realizing eschatology) coined by J. Jeremias in *Die Gleichnisse Jesu*, 2d ed. (Göttingen: Vandenhoeck und Ruprecht, 1952), though he does not endorse Jeremias's concept of the Kingdom. Realizing eschatology pictures the Kingdom as a dynamic force rather than as a state or condition.

14. On this see also *The Teaching of Jesus: Studies of Its Form and Content* (Cambridge: Cambridge University Press, 1931), 211–234; the quotation in the text is from p. 228. See also Manson's article "The Son of Man in Daniel, Enoch and the Gospels," *BJRL* 32 (1950), 171–193, reprinted in *Studies in the Gospels and the Epistles*, 123–145.

15. *Jesus and the Word* (Naperville, Ill.: Allenson, 1959), 8. The English translation was made in 1931 from the original edition, *Jesus* (Tübingen: J. C. B. Mohr, 1926).

16. James M. Robinson, the chronicler of the "new quest" (see below) characterizes Manson's position and that of V. Taylor and C. J. Cadoux in their articles in *ET* 52 (1941–1942) as "noteworthy for the unanimous rejection of the possibility of a real 'biography' and the almost equally unanimous assumption of a mediating position which is merely a sobered version of the original quest"—see *A New Quest of the Historical Jesus* (for details, see n. 17 below), p. 9, n. 2. See also my survey "Enige recente Studies over het Leven van Jezus," *Theologie en Praktijk* 15 (1955), 97–111, reporting on A. M. Hunter, *The Work and Words of Jesus* (1950); T. W. Manson, *The Servant-Messiah* (1953); V. Taylor, *The Life and Ministry of Jesus* (1954); H. E. W. Turner, *Jesus, Master and Lord* (1953); and J. W. C. Wand, *The Life of Jesus Christ* (1955).

17. In his *Essays on New Testament Themes* (Naperville, Ill.: Allenson, 1959), 15–47, translation of *Exegetische Versuche und Besinnungen* 1 (Göttingen: Vandenhoeck und Ruprecht, 1960), 187–213. The original article, "Das Problem des historischen Jesus," appeared in *ZTK* 51 (1954), 125–153. The first scholar to give a sketch of the new movement was J. M. Robinson in *A New Quest for the Historical Jesus* (SBT 25; London: SCM Press and Naperville, Ill.: Allenson, 1959).

18. First published in C. E. Braaten and Roy A. Harrisville, *Kerygma and*

*History* (Nashville: Abingdon, 1962), reprinted in N. A. Dahl, *The Crucified Messiah and Other Essays* (Minneapolis: Augsburg, 1974), 48–89 (the quotations below are from this collection of essays). The German version, "Der geschichtliche Jesus als geschichtswissenschaftliches und theologisches Problem," appeared in *Kerygma und Dogma* I (1955), 104–141. On its original setting see Dahl's preface to *The Crucified Messiah and Other Essays*, where he notes that "this paper was originally addressed to a Scandinavian audience and published in Norwegian before Ernst Käsemann's essay 'The Historical Jesus' initiated a heated debate" (8–9). This volume of essays also contains his well-balanced review of Bultmann's *Theologie des Neuen Testaments* (90–128), translated from an article in *Theologische Rundschau* 22 (1954), 21–49.

19. See also Dahl's "Anamnesis: Memory and Commemoration in Early Christianity" in another collection of essays, *Jesus in the Memory of the Early Church* (Minneapolis: Augsburg, 1976), 11–29. This was his inaugural lecture given at the University of Oslo in 1946. It was first published in French in *Studia Theologica* 1 (1948), 69–95.

20. See N. Perrin, *Rediscovering the Teaching of Jesus* (London: SCM Press and New York: Harper and Row, 1967), 45. Perrin, originally a student of T. W. Manson and J. Jeremias, wrote this book four years after his *The Kingdom of God in the Teaching of Jesus* (London: SCM Press and Philadelphia: Westminster Press, 1963), after having been converted to a form-critical view on the gospels. Hence his strong emphasis on "a methodology for reconstructing the teaching of Jesus, given this view of the sources" (11) in his first chapter (15–53). See also R. S. Barbour, *Traditio-Historical Criticism of the Gospels: Some Comments on Current Methods* (London: SPCK, 1972) and, very recently, M. E. Boring, "The Historical-Critical Method's 'Criteria of Authenticity': The Beatitudes in Q and Thomas as a Test Case," in C. W. Hedrick (ed.), *The Historical Jesus and the Rejected Gospels*, 9–44.

21. The classical definition, often quoted, is that by E. Käsemann: "Einigermassen sicheren Boden haben wir nur in einem einzigen Fall unter den Füssen, wenn nämlich Tradition aus irgendwelchen Gründen weder aus dem Judentum abgeleitet noch der Urchristenheit zugeschrieben werden kann, speziell dann, wenn die Juden-Christenheit ihr überkommenes Gut als zu kühn gemildert oder umgebogen hat" ("Das Problem des historischen Jesus," 235; "The Problem of the Historical Jesus," 37).

22. See note 10. The book goes back to a Cambridge Ph.D. dissertation prepared under C. F. D. Moule and submitted in 1969. See esp. chapter 6, "Jesus in the Gospel Traditions," and chapter 7 "The Gospel Traditions in the Early Church. In chapter 5 Stanton deals with "The Gospels and

Ancient Biographical Writings," a subject recently treated anew by D. E. Aune in *The New Testament and Its Literary Environment* (Philadelphia: Westminster Press, 1987), chapters 1 and 2. Another book worth mentioning is J. Roloff, *Das Kerygma und der historische Jesus: Historische Motive in den Jesus-Erzählungen der Evangelien* (Göttingen: Vandenhoeck und Ruprecht, 1970). Roloff analyzes significant examples of the narrative tradition concerning Jesus in order to show that looking back to Jesus' days on earth constituted an essential factor in the tradition process. Recollection was a central element in the formation of the kerygma from the very beginning (cf. Dahl).

23. In K. Kertelge (ed.), *Rückfrage nach Jesus: Zur Methodik und Bedeutung der Frage nach dem historischen Jesus* (QD 63; Freiburg: Herder, 1974), 11–77.

24. "Die vorösterlichen Anfänge der Logientradition," in H. Ristow and K. Matthiae, *Der historische Jesus und der kerygmatische Christus* (Berlin: Evangelische Verlagsanstalt, 1960), 342–370.

25. He refers several times to Dahl's publications; he could not know Stanton's work.

26. Here Hahn refers to the work of J. Jeremias left out of discussion in this book. See his "Kennzeichen der *ipsissima vox* Jesu," an article from 1954 now in *Abba: Studien zur neutestamentlichen Theologie und Zeitgeschichte* (Göttingen: Vandenhoeck und Ruprecht, 1966), 145–151, and *Neutestamentliche Theologie I: Die Verkündigung Jesu* (Gütersloh: Gerd Mohn, 1971), translated as *New Testament Theology, vol. 1: The Proclamation of Jesus* (New York: Charles Scribner's Sons, 1971), chapter 1.

27. Of course many more studies might have been discussed. Among the more recent ones I should like to single out E. P. Sanders, *Jesus and Judaism* (London: SCM Press and Philadelphia: Fortress Press, 1985) and R. Leivestad, *Jesus in His Own Perspective. An Examination of His Sayings, Actions and Eschatological Titles* ((Minneapolis: Augsburg, 1987).

28. See pp. 89–90 and the section "Ancient Elements in Acts?" (pp. 108–111).

29. See *Christology in Context*, 87–88.

30. On what follows see *Christology in Context*, 40–41, 53–57, 68–70.

31. Scholars differ on the originality of the phrase "the Son of God," and it is now usually placed in parentheses.

32. See *Christology in Context*, 53–57, 73–77, 84–88.

33. *A Future for the Historical Jesus: The Place of Jesus in Preaching and Theology* (Nashville and New York: Abingdon Press, 1971).

34. There are seven places where Paul uses the term "the Kingdom of God." In Rom. 14:17 he states that the Kingdom is concerned with righteousness, peace, and joy in the Holy Spirit; in 1 Cor. 6:9–10 and 15:50 and in Gal.

5:21 he speaks about inheriting the Kingdom (or failing to inherit it); in 1 Cor. 4:20 he underlines the dynamic character of the Kingdom; in 1 Cor. 15:24 he speaks about Christ handing over the Kingdom to God the Father; and in 1 Thess. 2:12 about God calling people to his Kingdom.

CHAPTER II: THEOLOGICAL CONSIDERATIONS IN THE
SEARCH FOR THE HISTORICAL JESUS

1. On this see my *Jesus: Inspiring and Disturbing Presence*, 38–41.
2. See *Jesus: Inspiring and Disturbing Presence*, 43–45, referring to Barth's chapter on D. F. Strauss in his *Protestant Theology in the Nineteenth Century* (London: SCM Press, 1972), 541–568. The original German edition gives the text of lectures given in 1932–1933.
3. New York: Charles Scribner's Sons, 1958. The German text is given in *Jesus Christus und die Mythologie* (Hamburg: Furche Verlag, 1964).
4. *Kerygma and historischer Jesus*, 2d ed. (Zurich and Stuttgart: Zwingli-Verlag, 1967).
5. Now brought together in W. G. Kümmel, *Dreissig Jahre Jesus-Forschung, 1950–1980* (BBB 60; Königstein im Taunus and Bonn: Peter Hanstein Verlag, 1985). This volume, edited by H. Merklein, runs to some 550 pages. Kümmel continues his reporting; see his "Jesus-Forschung seit 1981. I Forschungsgeschichte. Methodenfrage," *Theologische Rundschau* 53 (1988), 229–249.
6. See chapter 1, note 33. On what follows see also my articles "Nieuwe Bijdragen tot de Leben-Jesus-Forschung in Duitsland, *Vox Theologica* 29 (1959), 129–144; "Bultmann en Ebeling," *Theologie en Praktijk* 24 (1964), 70–86; and "Theologie als Hermeneutiek," in G. C. Berkouwer and A. S. van der Woude (eds.), *Revolte in de Theologie* (Nijkerk: G. F. Callenbach, 1968), 74–89. Cf. "The Inquiry After the Man Jesus of Nazareth," in *Jesus: Inspiring and Disturbing Presence*.
7. *Das Verhältnis der urchristlichen Christusbotschaft zum historischen Jesus* (Sitzungsberichte der Heidelberger Akademie der Wissenschaften, Phil.-Hist. Klasse 1960, 3; Heidelberg: Carl Winter, Universitätsverlag, 1962), translated as "The Primitive Christian Kerygma and the Historical Jesus," in C. E. Braaten and R. A. Harrisville (eds.), *The Historical Jesus and the Kerygmatic Christ* (Nashville: Abingdon Press, 1964), 15–42.
8. See his "The Problem of the Historical Jesus" and also his "Blind Alleys in the 'Jesus of History' Controversy," in *New Testament Questions of Today* (London: SCM Press and Philadelphia: Fortress, 1969), 23–65, translation

of "Sackgassen im Streit um den historischen Jesus," in *Exegetische Versuche und Besinnungen II* (Göttingen: Vandenhoeck und Ruprecht, 1964), 31–68.

9. Stuttgart: W. Kohlhammer, 1956, translated as *Jesus of Nazareth* (New York: Harper and Row, 1960).

10. *Das Verhältnis der urchristlichen Christusbotschaft zum historischen Jesus*, 12–13.

11. See Fuchs's article "Die Frage nach dem historischen Jesus," *ZTK* 53 (1956), 210–229; now in his *Zur Frage nach dem historischen Jesus* (Tübingen: J. C. B. Mohr, 1960), 143–167; translated as *Studies of the Historical Jesus* (London: SCM Press, and Naperville, Ill.: Allenson, 1964, 11–32). The quotations in the text are from pp. 21 and 25.

12. *Das Verhältnis der urchristlichen Christusbotschaft zum historischen Jesus*, 18–19. On Ebeling, see pp. 19–21.

13. See chapter 3, "Kerygma und historischer Jesus," pp. 19–82, in his *Theologie und Verkündigung: Ein Gespräch mit Rudolf Bultmann* (Tübingen: J. C. B. Mohr, 1962), translated as *Theology and Proclamation* (Philadelphia: Fortress Press, 1966), 32–81. The expressions "Witness of Faith" and "Ground of Faith" occur as chapter headings in *The Nature of Faith* (Philadelphia: Fortress Press, 1961), translation of *Das Wesen des christlichen Glaubens* (Tübingen: J. C. B. Mohr, 1959).

14. London: SCM Press, 1963. See also my "Search for a Modern Christology," chapter 4 of *Jesus: Inspiring and Disturbing Presence*, 56–71.

15. See, e.g., T. W. Manson's sharp comments in his review of the first part of the *Theologie des Neuen Testaments* in *JTS* 50 (1949), 202–206, which show little understanding for the theological problems raised by Bultmann.

16. New York: Harper and Row, 1964 (English edition *Early Christian Rhetoric: The Language of the Gospel* [London: SCM Press, 1964]). See especially chapter 8, "Language, Symbol and Myth," 126–136. On Wilder see also "Theology as Narration," chapter 6 of *Jesus: Inspiring and Disturbing Presence*, 86–98.

17. See also *Christology in Context*, 26–29.

CHAPTER III: JESUS' MISSION AND HIS DEATH ON THE CROSS

1. Concentration on and critical sifting of the synoptic material is found in Heinz Schürmann's thorough and stimulating collection of essays *Jesu ureigener Tod: Exegetische Besinnungen und Ausblick* (Freiburg-Basel-Wien: Herder, 1975) and *Gottes Reich—Jesu Geschick: Jesu ureigener Tod im Licht seiner Basileia-Verkündigung* (Freiburg: Herder, 1983). Also P. Pokorný, in

his *The Genesis of Christology: Foundations for a Theology of the New Testament* (Edinburgh: T. and T. Clark, 1987; translation of *Die Entstehung der Christologie*, Berlin: Evangelische Verlagsanstalt, 1985), speaks about Jesus of Nazareth (pp. 14–62) before dealing with the oldest testimonies of faith in the long section that bears the title "The Decisive Impulse" (pp. 63–167).

2. See also *Christology in Context*, chapter 11, "Jesus' Death, Resurrection and Exaltation" (pp. 173–188), and the section "Jesus' Death on the Cross" (pp. 208–211) in chapter 13, "The One with Whom It All Began"; cf. my article "Jesus' Death for Others and the Death of the Maccabean Martyrs," in T. Baarda, A. Hilhorst, G. P. Luttikhuizen, A. S. van der Woude (eds.), *Text and Testimony: Essays in honour of A. F. J. Klijn* (Kampen: Kok, 1988), pp. 142–151. A very good survey of the available material is given in M. L. Gubler, *Die frühesten Deutungen des Todes Jesu: Eine motivgeschichtliche Darstellung aufgrund der neueren exegetischen Forschung* (OBO 15; Freiburg: Universitätsverlag and Göttingen: Vandenhoeck und Ruprecht, 1977).

3. Because Paul is following a traditional line of argument for a moment, he says more than is strictly necessary in this context. It is noteworthy that he starts by speaking about the Jews in Judaea but finally includes all Jews who oppose his preaching to the Gentiles. He adds, "oppose all men," a standard feature of pagan anti-Jewish sentiment. I see no reason to regard these verses, or part of them, as a later interpolation. See the well-documented article by T. Baarda, "Maar de toorn is over hen gekomen (1 Thess. 2:16c)," in T. Baarda et al., *Paulus en de andere Joden: Exegetische Bijdragen en Discussie* (Delft: Meinema, 1984), 15–74.

4. In his very detailed study *Israel und das gewaltsame Geschick der Propheten: Untersuchungen zur Überlieferung des deuteronomistischen Geschichtsbildes im Alten Testament, Spätjudentum und Urchristentum* (WMANT 23; Neukirchen-Vluyn: Neukirchener Verlag, 1967).

5. The contrast-pattern employed in the speeches in Acts (e.g., in Acts 2:23–24: "This Jesus . . . you crucified and killed by the hand of lawless men. But God raised him up") also emphasizes the responsibility of the Jewish leaders for Jesus' death. It adds a resurrection formula, stressing God's initiative in raising Jesus from the dead. For details see my *Christology in Context*, 108–111.

6. Cf. also Mark 10:35–45 and par.

7. *Jesus and the Gospel Tradition* (London: SPCK, 1967), 76. This book gives the text of the Shaffer Lectures for 1965.

8. See my *Christology in Context*, 175–179, and in particular the interesting studies of L. Ruppert, *Der leidende Gerechte: Eine motivgeschichtliche Untersuchung zum Alten Testament und zwischentestamentlichen Judentum* (For-

schung zur Bibel 5; Würzburg: Echter Verlag, 1973); idem, *Jesus als der leidende Gerechte? Der Weg Jesu im Lichte eines alt- und zwischentestamentlichen Motivs* (SBS 59; Stuttgart: Katholisches Bibelwerk, 1972); and K. Th. Kleinknecht, *Der leidende Gerechtfertigte: Die alttestamentlich-jüdische Tradition vom 'leidenden Gerechten' und ihre Rezeption bei Paulus* (WUNT II, 13; Tübingen: J. C. B. Mohr, 1984).

9. George W. E. Nickelsburg, Jr., *Resurrection, Immortality, and Eternal Life in Intertestamental Judaism* (HTS 26; Cambridge: Harvard University Press and London: Oxford University Press, 1972), 88; see the entire section on the Book of Wisdom and related texts on pp. 48–92.

10. George W. E. Nickelsburg, in "The Genre and Function of the Markan Passion Narrative" (*HTR* 73 [1980], 153–184), has tried to demonstrate in detail that the pre-Markan passion narrative "recounted the death and exaltation of Jesus, employing the genre of the story of the righteous one" (p. 183). In his excursus "Die vormarkinische Passionsgeschichte," found on pp. 1–27 of his *Das Markusevangelium, II. Teil* (HTKNT II, 2; Freiburg: Herder, 1977), Rudolf Pesch has given two pages of possible allusions and references in the pre-Markan history of the passion (to which, according to him, much between 8:27 and 16:8 may be reckoned). His conclusion is that "zwei Drittel des Materials der vormk. Passionsgeschichte ist durch Anspielungen bzw. Zitationen von *passio-iusti*-Motiven ausgeprägt" (p. 13). This is no doubt exaggerated.

11. See "The Genre and Function of the Markan Passion Narrative," 183.

12. Here Nestle-Aland (26th ed.) has *hyper*, whereas Nestle-Aland (25th ed.) preferred *peri* with the original text of the Sinaiticus, the Vaticanus, and Minuscule 33 (with no change of meaning). Compare also 1 Pet. 2:21, "Christ suffered for you," and 3:18, "Christ . . . suffered for sins once and for all." "Suffered" (*epathen*) is very similar to "died" (*apethanen*). In fact, in 1 Pet. 3:18 Nestle-Aland (25th ed.) preferred the latter word, which also occurs as a variant in 1 Pet. 2:21 in a considerable number of witnesses. See also Phil. 1:29, where the expression "to suffer for Christ's sake" is used.

13. See also John 11:50, 51; 18:14.

14. See *Christology in Context*, 42, referring to W. A. Meeks, *The First Urban Christians: The Social World of the Apostle Paul* (New Haven and London: Yale University Press, 1983), 150–157: "Baptism: Ritual of Initiation."

15. In my contribution to the Klijn festschrift (*Text and Testimony*) I have argued that there is no reason to connect this verse with Jewish traditions concerning the "binding of Isaac" based on Gen. 22:1–19; see "Jesus' death for others," 146–147. See also *Christology in Context*, 241, note 36.

16. For details see J. W. van Henten, *De joodse martelaren als grondleggers van een*

*nieuwe orde* (Diss. Leiden, 1986); M. Hengel, *The Atonement: The Origins of the Doctrine in the New Testament* (London: SCM Press, 1981); and S. K. Williams, *Jesus' Death as Saving Event: The Background and Origin of a Concept* (HDR 2; Missoula, Mont.: Scholars Press, 1975).

17. So M. Hengel, *The Atonement*, 2–4, 60–61, against especially K. Wengst, *Christologische Formel und Lieder des Urchristentums* (SNT 7; Gütersloh: Gerd Mohn, 1972).

18. *antipsuchon autōn.*

19. Here again *antipsuchon* is used, this time with the genitive *tēs tou ethnous hamartias.*

20. *tou hilastēriou;* cf. Rom. 3:25.

21. In some ways the terminology with regard to the concept of vicarious expiatory death in 4 Maccabees is more explicit than that in 2 Maccabees, but the underlying idea is the same. The relatively late date of 4 Maccabees (on this, see J. W. van Henten, *De joodse martelaren,* 187–191, and his "Datierung und Herkunft des Vierten Makkabäerbuches," in J. W. van Henten et al. (eds.), *Tradition and Re-interpretation in Jewish and Early Christian Literature: Essays in Honour of Jürgen C. H. Lebram* [SPB 36; Leiden: E. J. Brill, 1986], 136–149) does not preclude using it as a source of parallels for early Christian ideas. The terms used in 4 Maccabees may be older than the writing itself.

22. See J. W. van Henten, *De joodse martelaren,* 138–144.

23. Compare the voluntary death of Taxo and his seven sons in As. Mos. 9 in order that their blood be avenged before the Lord, which is immediatedly followed by the appearance of God's Kingdom throughout his whole creation in chapter 10.

24. See also H. Schürmann, "Jesu ureigenes Todesverständnis," in *Gottes Reich—Jesu Geschick,* esp. 198–223. N. A. Dahl considers it probable that "Jesus not only foresaw his own death, but actually ascribed to it a vicarious significance and saw it as a necessary presupposition for the coming of the Kingdom of God if not his own enthronement as Son of man ("The Problem of the Historical Jesus," 75).

25. So C. K. Barrett in his foreword (p. ix) to Morna D. Hooker, *Jesus and the Servant: The Influence of the Servant Concept of Deutero-Isaiah in the New Testament* (London: SPCK, 1959).

26. See his article *"Pais theou,"* in *TWNT* 5 (1954), 653–713 = *TDNT* 5, 654–717 (cf. the reworked article *"Pais theou* im Neuen Testament," in *Abba: Studien zur neutestamentlichen Theologie und Zeitgeschichte* [Göttingen: Vandenhoeck und Ruprecht, 1966], 191–216). Compare his *New Testament*

*Theology. Vol. 1. The Proclamation of Jesus* London: SCM Press, and New York: Charles Scribner's Sons, 1971), § 24, 2, "The Interpretation of Suffering," translation of *Neutestamentliche Theologie. I. Die Verkündigung Jesu* (Gütersloh: Gerd Mohn, 1971), § 24, 2 "Die Leidensdeutung" (272–284).

27. *The Christology of the New Testament,* 2d ed. (Philadelphia: Westminster Press, 1959, 1963), 51–82, translation of *Die Christologie des Neuen Testaments* (Tübingen: J. C. B. Mohr, 1957), 50–81. For further advocates of this view (and others) see chapter 1 (1–24) in M. D. Hooker's *Jesus and the Servant* and H. Haag, *Der Gottesknecht bei Deuterojesaja* (Darmstadt: Wiss. Buchgesellschaft, 1985), 66–79.

28. "The Background of Mark 10:45" in A. J. B. Higgins (ed.), *New Testament Essays: Studies in Memory of T. W. Manson, 1893–1958* (Manchester: Manchester University Press, 1959), 1–18. See also his *Jesus in the Gospel Tradition,* 39–41.

29. *The Atonement,* 59.

30. Ibid.

31. On this see also *Christology in Context,* 179–181, and "Jesus' Death for Others and the Death of the Maccabean Martyrs" (see note 2), 146. Also Schürmann, *Gottes Reich—Jesu Geschick,* 236–241, comes to a negative conclusion.

32. "I should like to suggest that there is in the Enoch picture a double oscillation, so to speak, for which there are parallels elsewhere. The group idea finds expression in the concept of the elect and righteous ones, i.e. the Israel within Israel, the Remnant. The individual idea finds expression in two personalities: at the beginning of the course of events in Enoch, who is regarded as the first human being to embody the Son of Man idea, the nucleus of the group of elect and righteous ones; at the end it finds expression again in the figure of the Messiah who is to carry out the final vindication of the saints. But whether it be in Enoch, who is as it were the first-born of many brethren, or in the Messiah, or in the corporate body of the elect and righteous, it is the same idea that is embodied, an idea that formed part of the divine purpose before the creation of the world." ("The Son of Man in Daniel, Enoch and the Gospels," as reprinted in *Studies in the Gospels and Epistles,* 140–141).

33. "The Son of Man in Daniel, Enoch and the Gospels," 143.

34. Ibid., 143–145. Cf. J. Jeremias, *TWNT* 5, 687: "Die damit erstmalig [in the Parables of Enoch] vollzogene Kombination von Menschensohn und Gottesknecht ist für das Sendungsbewusstsein Jesu von entscheidender Bedeutung gewesen"; translation, with a significant addition, in *TDNT* 5, 688:

"The resultant combination of the Son of Man and the servant of God, though restricted to traits which exalt the servant's glory, was of decisive significance for Jesus' sense of mission."

35. See his *Jesus and the Gospel Tradition,* 41–45 and 89–97. On p. 41 he says (without mentioning Manson): "And to interpret 'Son of man' as if this title were simply a cypher for 'Servant of the Lord' is methodically illegitimate.

36. London: SPCK, 1967. See also her contribution, "Is the Son of Man Problem Really Insoluble?" in E. Best and R. McL. Wilson (eds.), *Text and Interpretation: Studies in the New Testament Presented to Matthew Black* (Cambridge: Cambridge University Press, 1979), 155–168. Cf. C. F. D. Moule, *The Origin of Christology* (Cambridge: Cambridge University Press, 1977), 22–30.

37. *The Son of Man in Mark,* 190.

38. On what follows, see also *Christology in Context,* 58–59, 77–79, 86, 169–172, 207. For a survey of recent opinions see A. Yarbro Collins, "The Origin of the Designation of Jesus as 'Son of Man,'" *HTR* 80 (1987), 391–407; she does not, however, refer to the studies mentioned here. Yarbro Collins considers it likely that "Jesus spoke of a heavenly Son of Man and that, after his death and presuming his exaltation, some of his followers identified him in his exalted state with that being" (p. 404). See also G. W. E. Nickelsburg's article "Son of Man" in *Anchor Bible Dictionary* (forthcoming; the author kindly put it at my disposal), especially also for the Old Testament and Jewish background of the term.

39. An exception is John 5:27. The Greek expression is *ho huios tou anthrōpou,* in which the second noun has the article in accordance with New Testament Greek usage. M. Hengel has argued that this uniform rendering of an Aramaic term points to an early translation of the Jesus tradition at a particular place; see his *Between Jesus and Paul: Studies in the Earliest History of Christianity* (London: SCM Press, 1983), 27–28. C. F. D. Moule, *The Origin of Christology,* 13, has argued that the definite article was used because the term wanted to refer expressly to Daniel's Son of man.

40. It continues to play an important role in the Fourth Gospel, for instance.

41. See, e.g., G. Vermes, *Jesus the Jew: A Historian's Reading of the Gospels* 2d ed., (London: Collins, 1973, 1977), 160–191; J. A. Fitzmyer, "The New Testament Title 'Son of Man' Philologically Considered," in *A Wandering Aramean: Collected Aramaic Essays* (SBLMonS 25; Missoula, Mont.: Scholars Press, 1979), 143–160; M. Casey, *Son of Man: The Interpretation and Influence of Daniel 7* (London: SPCK, 1979); and B. Lindars, *Jesus, Son of Man: A Fresh Examination of the Son of Man Sayings in the Gospel in the Light of Recent Research* (London: SPCK, 1983).

42. This is brought out clearly by J. D. Kingsbury in chapter 4 (pp. 157–179) of *The Christology of Mark's Gospel* (Philadelphia: Fortress Press, 1983).

43. So, e.g., M. A. Knibb, "The Date of the Parables of Enoch: A Critical Review," *NTS* 25 (1978–79), 345–359. A complicating factor is that the Parables have been preserved only in Ethiopic; no Greek or Aramaic fragments have come down to us.

44. G. N. Stanton has correctly stressed that Jesus' interpretation of the designation Son of man and his proclamation of God's Kingdom were juxtaposed and could be linked together. "Jesus saw himself as the obedient, faithful yet rejected and suffering Son of Man who would be vindicated by God; Jesus taught that God's rule was already manifesting itself in his ministry and person, even though it was also yet to come" (p. 165). Both important themes were, of course, directly related to Jesus' person and his actions.

CHAPTER IV: JESUS AS INAUGURATOR OF THE KINGDOM

1. "Die Auferweckung Jesu und die Anfänge der Christologie (Messias bzw. Sohn Gottes und Menschensohn)," *ZNW* 72 (1981), 1–26, now in H. Merklein, *Studien zu Jesus und Paulus* (WUNT 43; Tübingen: J. C. B. Mohr, 1987), 221–246. The statements relevant to our present purpose are found on pp. 1–4 (221–224). See also Merklein's notes for the views of other interpreters.

2. See also *Christology in Context*, 37–38.

3. Merklein rejects K. Berger's theory that the resurrection of Jesus should be viewed against the background of Jewish notions about the death and resurrection of (a) final, eschatological prophet(s). In his voluminous study *Die Auferstehung des Propheten und die Erhöhung des Menschensohnes: Traditionsgeschichtliche Untersuchungen zur Deutung des Geschickes Jesu in frühchristlichen Texten* (SUNT 13; Göttingen: Vandenhoeck und Ruprecht, 1976), Berger has brought together a wealth of interesting material to support his thesis. The central question is, however, how many of the parallels taken mainly from late texts of Christian origin (or at least handed down by Christians) can really prove what they are supposed to prove. Central to Berger's argument are, e.g., Mark 6:14 and Rev. 11:1–13. We shall be wise to concentrate on the traditions concerning suffering righteous servants and martyrs (which also play a role in Berger's argumentation).

4. As is clear from many studies devoted to the subject; see those mentioned by Merklein in his note 9 and H. C. C. Cavallin, *Life after Death I* (CBNT 7, 1; Lund: C. W. K. Gleerup, 1977).

5. In his *Jesus' Predictions of Vindication and Resurrection: The Provenance, Mean-*

*ing and Correlation of the Synoptic Predictions* (WUNT II 20, Tübingen: J. C. B. Mohr, 1986), H. F. Bayer speaks of the "opalescent meaning of 'resurrection' in the first part of the first century A.D." (25).

6. See "The Decisive Impulse," chapter 3 of *The Genesis of Christology;* quotation from p. 128.

7. The word *later* has to be seen in light of Pokorný's argument in an earlier section of his work to which he refers here ("The Positive Sign," pp. 114–119). There he distinguishes a stage in which the eschatological ecstatic joy predominated over other expressions of faith from a later one in which the acclamations and confessional phrases are first formulated. He emphasizes that Christian worship continued to contain an element of anticipation of eschatological happiness and that formulaic expressions were contained within the structure of primitive Christian joy (see esp. pp. 117–118).

8. (Edinburgh: T. and T. Clark, 1987). Originally published by Fortress Press, Philadelphia (1985).

9. See his chapter 2, "The Great Tribulation in Jewish Literature" (5–25).

10. See P. Volz, *Die Eschatologie der jüdischen Gemeinde im neutestamentlichen Zeitalter* (Tübingen: J. C. B. Mohr, 1934, Reprint Hildesheim: G. Olms, 1966), § 31, "Die letzte böse Zeit" (pp. 147–163; on p. 147 there is a small excursus on the expression "the woes of the Messiah"). Cf. also Allison, p. 6, n. 6.

11. See his chapter 6, "The Pauline Epistles" (62–69).

12. J. Christiaan Beker, *Paul the Apostle: The Triumph of God in Life and Thought* (Philadelphia: Fortress Press, 1980), 145–146: "Christians do not simply 'endure' the tribulations of the end time and do not simply 'wait' for the end of suffering in God's glorious new age. Christians can already 'glory' in sufferings (Rom. 5:3), because God's power manifests itself in the midst of suffering."

13. See chapter 11 "The Death of Jesus and the Great Tribulation" (115–141), where he mentions, e.g., Luke 12:51–53, par. Matt. 10:34–36 (Q); Matt. 11:12–13, par. Luke 16:16 (Q); Mark 3:27; Luke 12:49–50, as well as sayings concerning the suffering of Jesus and his disciples and their vindication. The authenticity and exact meaning of these passages cannot be discussed here.

14. See *The Quest of the Historical Jesus*, as discussed in chapter 1 of this book.

15. See the entire section on "Son of man" (128–137). Referring to T. W. Manson's view, Allison considers it likely that "when Jesus spoke of the Son of man he had in view a community at whose head he saw himself: a corporate personality embodied most fully in his own person."

16. Paul specifies: "For the trumpet will sound, and the dead will be raised

imperishable, and we shall be changed. For this perishable nature must put on the imperishable, and this mortal nature must put on immortality" (1 Cor. 15:52–53, cf. vv. 50–51 and 1 Thess. 4:13–18).

17. See H. F. Bayer, *Jesus' Predictions of Vindication and Resurrection,* p. 256: "Jesus' anticipation of the parousia is clearly distinguishable from his anticipation of vindication and resurrection. While the question of near-expectation remains open, a clear distinction between the categories or parousia and resurrection is traceable to the earliest strands of tradition and discourages the idea of the interchangeability of the two concepts."

18. See Dahl, "The Problem of the Historical Jesus," p. 82 (already quoted in chapter 1).

19. On this, see my Groningen lecture *De Toekomstverwachting in de Psalmen van Salomo* (Leiden: E. J. Brill, 1965), 16–17, now translated as "The Expectation of the Future in the Psalms of Solomon," *Neotestamentica* 23 (1989), 93–117; see esp. 99–100.

20. On this, see also my *Christology in Context,* 115–120.

21. Most easily accessible in his *Studien zu Jesus und Paulus* (see note 1 of this chapter), 127–156; the reference in the text is to p. 130. See also his books *Die Gottesherrschaft als Handlungsprinzip* (Forschung zur Bibel 34; Würzburg: Echter Verlag, 1978), and especially *Jesu Botschaft von der Gottesherrschaft: Eine Skizze* (SBS 111; Stuttgart: Katholisches Bibelwerk, 1983).

22. See also Wilder's article "Eschatological Imagery and Earthly Circumstance," *NTS* 5 (1958–1959), 229–245. See especially p. 231: "The eschatological myth dramatizes the transfiguration of the world and is not a mere poetry of an unthinkable a-temporal state" and p. 232: "the characteristic imagery everywhere suggests a renewed or fulfilled creation, not an a-cosmic state."

23. So my summary on p. 206 of *Christology in Context;* see the entire section on "Jesus and the Kingdom of God" (pp. 205–208).

24. See in particular G. R. Beasley-Murray, *Jesus and the Kingdom of God* (Grand Rapids: Eerdmans and Exeter: Paternoster Press, 1986).

25. On these questions see E. P. Sanders, *Jesus and Judaism,* Part Three, "Conflict and Death" (244–318). On p. 267 he writes: "Thus one can understand why scholars speak of Jesus' 'sovereign freedom' over the law. He apparently did not think that it could be freely transgressed, but rather that it was not final. This attitude almost certainly sprang from his conviction that the new age was at hand."

26. See also R. Leivestad, *Jesus in His Own Perspective:* "it is doubtful that there is any authentic tradition which makes the person of Jesus central, to the extent that it is *he* who acts as saviour or judge, and it is *he* upon whom

people's fate depends. That which determines salvation or condemnation is whether one receives the message of the Kingdom of God and becomes obedient to God, not whether one associates with the man Jesus" (p. 120).

27. See Schweizer's *Jesus* (London: SCM Press and Richmond: John Knox, 1971), 21, 22. In the German original, *Jesus Christus im vielfältigen Zeugnis des Neuen Testaments* (Munich and Hamburg: Siebenstern Taschenbuch Verlag, 1968), 25–26: "So oder so hat Jesus jedenfalls keinen gängigen Titel im Sinne einer Hoheitsaussage aufgenommen" but "Jesus hielt das Feld offen, ohne durch Titel, die notwendig immer fixieren und ausschliessen, Gottes freies Handeln so zum Objekt menschlichen Denkens werden zu lassen, dass dieses darüber verfügen könnte."

28. See also *Jesu Botschaft von der Gottesherrschaft*, 83–91.

29. See "Die Auferweckung Jesu und die Anfänge der Christologie," p. 221 (especially note 4) and also "Jesus, Künder des Reiches Gottes," 153–154; *Jesu Botschaft von der Gottesherrschaft*, 145–171.

30. See, e.g., the three recent "Christologies of the New Testament" that take the titles as their starting point: O. Cullmann, *The Christology of the New Testament*, 2d ed. (Philadelphia: Westminster Press, 1963); F. Hahn, *The Titles of Jesus in Christology: Their History in Early Christianity* (London: Lutterworth and New York: World Publishing Co, 1969), translation of *Christologische Hoheitstitel: Ihre Geschichte im frühen Christentum* (FRLANT 83; Göttingen: Vandenhoeck und Ruprecht, 1963), and R. H. Fuller, *The Foundations of New Testament Christology* (London: Lutterworth and New York: Charles Scribner's Sons, 1965).

31. So also recently G. R. Beasley-Murray in his *Jesus and the Kingdom* at the end of an interesting excursus, "The Relation of Jesus to the Kingdom of God in the Present" (144–146). Here he calls Jesus the "Champion or Contender for the Kingdom of God" (Mark 3:27), "Initiator of the Kingdom" (Matt. 11:12), "Instrument of the Kingdom" (Matt. 12:28), "Representative of the Kingdom of God" (Luke 17:20–21), "Mediator of the Kingdom" (Mark 2:18–19), "Bearer of the Kingdom" (Matt. 11:5), and "Revealer of the Kingdom" (Matt. 13:16–17). He concludes, "Since we would do well to have a term to denote the manifold function of Jesus with respect to the Kingdom of God, and since the title *Messiah* is the acknowledged umbrella term to denote the representative of the Kingdom, it is difficult to avoid appropriating it for Jesus" (p. 146). Comparable is P. Pokorný's use of the term. Commenting on the fact that the expectation of the resurrection of many was fulfilled in the resurrection of one person Jesus, he says: "It follows that everybody's future is dependent on this man. The concretisation implies the representative status of this one person, as the

simple statements of faith already indicate. . . . If only one person has risen, he must be the Messiah" (*The Genesis of Christology*, p. 138).

32. See my articles "The Use of the Word 'Anointed' in the Time of Jesus," *NovT* 8 (1966), 132–148, and "The Earliest Christian Use of *Christos: Some Suggestions*," *NTS* 32 (1986), 321–343. What follows in this section can be found in more detail in the latter article; cf. *Christology in Context*, 166–167, 208–211.

33. See "The Messiahship of Jesus in Paul," in *The Crucified Messiah and Other Essays*, 37–47, translation of "Die Messianität Jesu bei Paulus," in *Studia Paulina in honorem Johannis de Zwaan* (Haarlem: Erven F. Bohn, 1953), 83–95. The quotation in the text is from p. 40.

34. In *The Crucified Messiah and Other Essays*, 10–36. It goes back to "Der gekreuzigte Messias," in H. Ristow and K. Matthiae (eds.), *Der historische Jesus und der kerygmatische Christus* (Berlin: Evangelische Verlagsanstalt, 1960), 149–169.

35. On the same page he writes: "Jewish messianic expectations do not explain the meaning of the name Messiah assigned to Jesus. Neither can it be said that the title Messiah is the necessary contemporary expression for the conviction that Jesus is the eschatological bringer of salvation. This is no more valid than the older assertion that messiahship was the necessary garb for the archetypal religious self-consciousness of Jesus."

36. So also Ragnar Leivestad, *Jesus in His Own Perspective*, 95–96. In my article "The Earliest Use of *Christos:* Some Suggestions" I was not aware of the fact that Leivestad had also criticized Dahl on this point in the original Norwegian version of his book, which appeared in 1982.

37. Cf. the ancient formula in Rom. 1:3–4 "descended from David according to the flesh and designated Son of God in power according to the Spirit of holiness by his resurrection from the dead."

38. See M.-A. Chevallier, *L'Esprit et le Messie dans le Bas-Judaisme et le Nouveau Testament* (Paris: Presses Universitaires de France, 1958).

39. R. Leivestad, *Jesus in His Own Perspective*, 99–100, pointing only to 1 Sam. 16:13, does not go far enough when he speaks of Jesus, as *messias designatus*. David was anointed long before he assumed his kingdom "in power"; yet he is clearly "the Lord's anointed" from the very moment Samuel has anointed him (1 Sam. 16:6–13).

40. Helmut Merklein is of this opinion, together with many other scholars; see "Die Auferweckung Jesu und die Anfänge der Christologie," esp. pp. 224–236. According to Merklein, the oldest explicit Christology is that which connects resurrection and enthronement (Mark 14:61–62; Rom. 1:3–4; 1 Thess. 1:9–10; Acts 2:32–36; 13:33). Ferdinand Hahn went even farther

and assumed that the title Messiah was originally connected with the parousia (see *The Titles of Jesus in Christology,* 162).

41. On this see also *Christology in Context,* 167–169, 207–208.

42. See also *Christology in Context,* 42–43, 190–194.

43. This psalm verse is also quoted in Heb. 5:5 and 1:5 (there together with 2 Sam. 7:14; cf. Luke 1:32–33). See also Acts 2:32–36.

44. Cf. 4 QFlor 1:7–11, quoting from 2 Sam. 7:11–14 in connection with the "Branch of David," and 4 QpsDanAᵃ.

45. So, e.g., M. Hengel, *The Son of God* (Philadelphia: Fortress Press and London: SCM Press, 1976), 63–64, translation of *Der Sohn Gottes* (Tübingen: J. C. B. Mohr, 1975), 100–101. Hengel refers here to O. Betz and E. Schweizer.

46. On this see especially J. D. Kingsbury, *The Christology of Mark's Gospel* (Philadelphia: Fortress Press, 1983), 60–68. See also Mark 13:32. Mark begins his book with the sentence "The beginning of the gospel of Jesus Christ, the Son of God" (1:1), but here, as is well known, it is doubtful whether "Son of God" is original.

47. On the use of *abba* (and the recent research on it), see Joseph A. Fitzmyer's excellent contribution "*Abba* and Jesus' Relation to God" in *À Cause de l'Évangile: Études sur les Synoptiques et les Actes offerts à Dom Jacques Dupont* (Lectio Divina 123; Paris: Éditions du Cerf, 1985), 15–38.

48. On this see, again, Fitzmyer, especially pp. 35–38, and also the careful study of the passage by B. M. F. van Iersel in *'Der Sohn' in den synoptischen Jesusworten,* 2d ed. (NovT Sup 3; Leiden: E. J. Brill, 1964), 146–164.

EPILOGUE: JESUS AT THE CROSSROADS OF TRADITION

1. See "The Historical-Critical Method's 'Criteria of Authenticity'" (cited in chapter 1, note 20), 14.

# Index of Scriptural and Other Ancient Literatures

# General Index

Collins, Adela Yarbro, 96n38
Comparative study of religious con-
cepts, 30–31, 76
Corporate notions, 42–43, 57, 59; of
Son of man, 9, 50–51
Crossroads of traditions, Jesus at,
11, 76
Cross-section method, 11, 77
Cullmann, Oscar, 48, 100n30

Dahl, Nils A., 10–12, 27–29, 58,
61, 68–69, 77
Davies, William D., and Daube,
David, 86n6
David, Jesus as Son of, 70–72, 80
Death and resurrection: in pre-
Pauline formulas and Paul, 3, 17,
18, 42, 56–57, 81; for early
Christianity, 5, 12, 14, 27–28, 79,
81; and Jesus' life, 18, 32–33, 44–
45; complementary interpretations, 34; predictions in Mark,
38–39, 52, 61; and messianic
woes, 58–62
Death of Jesus, vii, 2, 42–48, 79; in
A. Schweitzer's view, 8; in Manson's view, 9; in early Christian
formulas, 17, 24, 32–34, 42, 72,
81; Jesus' own view of, 24–26,
32–54 passim, 55–56, 60–62;
effecting definitive change, 34, 36,
41, 44, 47, 55, 78; as death for
others, 42–48; and Maccabean
martyrs, 45–47; and the Suffering
Servant, 49
Demythologizing: 22; criticized by
A. N. Wilder, 29–30, 64. *See also*
Existential interpretation
Disciples of Jesus, 25–26, 36–38,
42, 51–52, 59, 61–62

Dodd, Charles H., 8, 64

Ebeling, Gerhard, 26
Envoy rejected by Israel: Jewish traditions, 36, 49, 53; Jesus as final
envoy, 16–17, 34–37, 78–79,
92n5
Eschatology: Jewish, 6, 8, 62–64; fu-
turistic/thoroughgoing, 8, 20, 62;
realized, 8, 64; in Wisd. Sol., 40;
realizing, 87n13
Eucharist. *See* Table of the Lord
Existential interpretation: of eschatological terms, 21–22, 25; of
Jesus' message, 21, 26; danger of
dehistoricizing, 28, 30. *See also*
Demythologizing
Existentialist kerygmatic theology,
21–22
Expiation/propitiation, 46, 94n21

Fitzmyer, Joseph A., 96n41, 102n47,
n48
Form criticism: 2–4, 20; Manson's
skepticism, 4–5; Dahl's strictures,
10–11
Fuchs, Ernst, 25–26
Fuller, Reginald H., 100n30

God's dealings with Israel and the
world: pivotal role of Jesus, 1–3,
6, 33, 75; especially Jesus' death
(and resurrection) 47, 55, 78
Gospel: traditions of, 13–15, 24–28;
"Gospel of Christ," 17–19
Gubler, Marie Louise, 92n2

Haag, Herbert, 95n27
Hahn, Ferdinand, 12–15, 58, 66,
89n26, 100n30, 101n40